The Art of Analyzing People

*Learn How to Analyze People
Through Gestures and Body Language*

**Author
AMANDA M. MYERS**

Copyright © 2019 by Amanda M. Myers - All rights reserved.

The content contained within this book may not be reproduced, duplicated or transmitted without direct written permission from the author or the publisher.

Under no circumstances will any blame or legal responsibility be held against the publisher, or author, for any damages, reparation, or monetary loss due to the information contained within this book, either directly or indirectly.

Legal Notice:

This book is copyright protected. It is only for personal use. You cannot amend, distribute, sell, use, quote or paraphrase any part, or the content within this book, without the consent of the author or publisher.

Disclaimer Notice:

Please note the information contained within this document is for educational and entertainment purposes only. All effort has been executed to present accurate, up to date, reliable, complete information. No warranties of any kind are declared or implied. Readers acknowledge that the author is not engaging in the rendering of legal, financial, medical or professional advice. The content within this book has been derived from various sources. Please consult a licensed professional before attempting any techniques outlined in this book.

By reading this document, the reader agrees that under no circumstances is the author responsible for any losses, direct or indirect, that are incurred as a result of the use of information contained within this document, including, but not limited to, errors, omissions, or inaccuracies.

Table of Contents

Introduction: The People Around You	1
Chapter 1: What Does it Mean to Analyze People?	3
Chapter 2: Why Learn How to Analyze People?	8
Chapter 3: The Benefits of Analyzing People	13
Chapter 4: Things to Keep in Mind	20
Chapter 5: The Basics	26
Chapter 6: Some of the Best Methods for Analyzing People	43
Chapter 7: The Art of Analyzing Others	60
Chapter 8: Things to Avoid while Analyzing Other People	86
Chapter 9: Learning How to Analyze Yourself	96
Chapter 10: Becoming a Master at Analyzing People	105
Conclusion: It's Time to Start Learning More About the People Around You	112
References	115

Introduction:
The People Around You

Whenever you meet someone new, what thoughts and feelings run through your mind? Do you simply smile, nod, and introduce yourself, or do you have a tendency to try and analyze everyone you meet? Whether you're the former or the latter, learning how to analyze people is an important skill which you can use in so many ways.

But when you think about it, is there some kind of standard method or formula to use which can help you understand others? According to experts, you can better understand the personality of a person based on their facial features, body language, and gestures. Although these factors are indeed very helpful, analyzing people requires more profound knowledge about other things. Fortunately, you will be learning all about these things throughout this book.

Being able to analyze people well can help you in many different aspects of your life. Professionally, analyzing people comes in handy, especially in cases when you're trying to decide whether to hire or promote an employee. This skill also comes in handy when you need to get to know some of your coworkers better. Personally, being able to analyze people can help you out a lot, too. Before you allow a person to become a part of your life, you must analyze them first to find out whether or not they're worth getting to know more. This skill has a lot of other practical applications which we will be discussing later on.

Learning how to analyze people is a process. It's not just about reading a comprehensive article then immediately knowing how to do it well. It's more about learning the basics and all other important information which will help guide you when you're faced with real-life situations. Apart from this, you also have to do a lot of practice and reflection if you really want to master this skill. With that being said, let's dive right into it!

Chapter 1:
What Does it Mean to Analyze People?

Before we go into the actual methods of analyzing people, let's first try to understand what it means to analyze others. Have you ever tried reading another person? How fast are you able to understand others right now? When it comes to this skill, the more you learn and practice, the better you get at it.

Basically, analyzing people means that you're trying to evaluate or assess them either upon meeting them or when you're trying to learn more about them. You can think of it like your own personal quest to get to know a person using your own observations, the interaction you've had with the person, and a number of effective methods which other people have developed and used for this same purpose.

Learning how to analyze others is a skill you can't develop unless you learn how to analyze yourself first. Unfortunately, this is a very difficult thing for most people. They try so hard to analyze others but when it comes to themselves, they remain clueless! You must first understand who you are, what you like, what you dislike, and what makes you tick. If you're able to analyze and understand yourself completely, you would have already won half the battle. Then when it's time for you to move on to others, here are some thoughts for you:

- **Consider the nature of those you're trying to analyze**

    This helps you understand their basic needs which, in turn, helps you read them better. Focus on what the other person does, especially during their free time. This says a lot about people. For instance, if you meet someone who does a lot of community service, this could mean two things—the person is either really interested in his community or he is more interested in his social status. If you want to find out which one is the truth, ask yourself questions such as:

    - Did this person grow up in this community?
    - What is the motivation of this person for participating actively in community activities?
    - Does this person need something?
    - Does this person lead an active social life?

    The questions to come up with would depend on the situation and on the person you're trying to analyze. The point is to think of questions which will help you learn more about the person based on his nature.

- **Focus on the body language of people**

    A person's body language can give you an idea of his inner mood. How people move when you talk to them or when you observe them from a distance can tell you more about them, too. Martha may always walk with her head up high, chest pointed out, and she always has a smile on her face. But when she walks, you notice that there's a certain stiffness to her gait. This may mean that, on the outside,

Martha may seem confident but when you consider the stiffness of her walk, this may be an indication of how she also feels self-conscious and she's afraid of being judged by others.

Then there's Charlie who always seems to be happy and even-tempered. He always walks with a "pep in his step" but he also tends to look down at the ground frequently. Although Charlie may be a happy person, his movements may indicate that he is also more of an introvert, especially when it comes to expressing his emotions to other people.

- **Focus on what people say, too**

When you are talking to another person, pay close attention to what he is talking about and what he is saying. Typically, people tend to talk a lot about the things which are most important to them. Going back to the example we used in the first point, let's assume that you have met two people—Charlie and Martha.

Both Charlie and Martha love doing community service and they are both active in community activities. When you talk to Martha, she talks about how many fundraising events she has organized, how many people she has helped, and how she loves interacting with others whenever she joins community activities. When you talk to Charlie, he talks about the people he has worked with, how helping others makes his life more meaningful, and his future plans to serve the community.

Based on what these people talk about, who do you think genuinely cares about the community and who cares more about social status? Although in this example the answer is quite obvious, there may be times when being able to analyze a person won't just be as simple as having a conversation with them. There are other things to consider as well.

- **Consider cultural differences**

    This part may be a bit trickier, especially if you don't have a lot of experience interacting with people of different cultures. In such a case, you may want to learn all that you can about the various cultures around the world, especially if you plan to become a master at analyzing people.

    As you're trying to analyze another person, you must consider his cultural background as well. The more you know about the person's culture, the more you will be able to analyze him effectively. Many times, when someone of a different culture acts differently, it's because that's normal in their culture!

Learning how to analyze people is a complicated task, but it's not an impossible one. There are a lot of tips, tricks, and strategies you can employ, but practicing this skill is important, too. The more you practice it, the better at it you'll get.

Is It Alright to Analyze Everyone You Meet?

Analyzing people is an important and useful skill to have. But is it alright to analyze each and every person you meet? This is one question that is frequently asked to psychiatrists, detectives, and other people whose professions require them to analyze people on a daily basis. For these people, it's part of their job to take one look at a person and try to analyze them. But if you're not really into the business of analyzing others, is it alright for you to do this?

Let's put this aside for a moment and try to look at this situation from a different perspective. Imagine an interior designer who has spent years studying for his craft and has been working as an interior designer for a few years now. Of course, this person would be going in and out of buildings, homes, and other structures every single day. Even without realizing it, this person may analyze the spaces he enters each day. This is especially true if he enters a space which is particularly beautiful or one which he finds unattractive. Normally though, he would relate to such spaces in the same way as everyone else.

Although it's perfectly alright for you to analyze everyone you meet, this doesn't mean that you have to do it. That is, unless you meet someone who is particularly interesting or if you have a specific reason for needing to analyze this person. After all, you might find it to be exhausting when you consciously try to analyze each and every new person you meet!

Chapter 2:
Why Learn How to Analyze People?

Being able to analyze or "read" people is a very valuable skill both in your professional and personal life. Each person you interact with sends signals. When you know what to listen and look for, each person will be telling you exactly how you can effectively work with or handle them. We all share the same basic needs which are recognition, relationships, regimentation, and results with some of these being more important to us than others. People have different personalities depending on which need they prioritize.

So why would you need (or want) to learn how to analyze people? There are many reasons why people embark on this learning journey. You may have your own personal reasons for why you want to acquire this skill. Before you actually start learning how to read people, you might first determine why you want this skill to be part of your arsenal. That way, when you're faced with challenges, you can remind yourself of your reason for learning which, in turn, helps you remain motivated to keep on learning and practicing until you have achieved mastery.

For now, let's take a look at some of the most common reasons why people decide to learn the art of analyzing people. You might discover that one or more of these reasons applies to you as well.

Genuine Interest

If you weren't genuinely interested in people, then you wouldn't have any interest in analyzing them as well. But if you have this genuine interest in why people behave the way they do or what pushes them to make decisions, then you would want to learn how to read them more effectively. Just because your profession doesn't require you to learn how to read people, that doesn't mean that you don't have the right to acquire this skill for yourself. As long as you find people interesting, learning how to analyze others also becomes an interesting subject for you.

A Desire to Understand Others

Even if you're not curious, you may have a strong desire to understand the people around you. There are times when you meet people who fascinate you so much that you want to learn more about them. But if don't get the chance to really sit down with this person or spend a lot of time with them, how will you get to know them better? One way to do this is to learn how to analyze others. There are certain things you can look out for in people which helps you learn more about them even without spending a lot of time with them. This is what makes the skill so appealing.

Awareness

Finally, you may also want to learn this skill in order to become more aware of the people you meet and interact with. Being able to read other people can help you determine whether they have good intentions or not. This can also help you understand why they behave in such a way or why they decided to deal with issues the way they did. Analyzing others gives you a different level of awareness which not all people possess.

Curiosity

This is probably the most common reason why people want to learn how to analyze others. Curiosity is a very powerful thing. When you feel curious about something, this may push you to start investigating why people act the way they do. If you're a curious person, you don't just take things at their face value. You always have this urge to dig a little deeper in order to get a more profound understanding of the people you meet and interact with. Of course, this doesn't always mean that when you are curious, you will be able to find all the reasons why things happen or why people are the way they are. But if you are curious, learning how to analyze people definitely becomes a skill you would like to learn.

To Deal with Pain

Your reason may also stem from personal experience. Perhaps there was someone in your life who has caused you pain or grief and you don't understand how this could have happened. In order to deal with your pain, you start learning how to analyze people better. That way, you will be able to determine whether a person is worth investing your time and effort in early on. Although the strategies for analyzing people aren't completely foolproof, they can still help you out in the long-run.

An Attempt to Let Go

This is another common reason which stems from an emotional reaction. Usually, this reason would come from people who have been hurt by someone and who are finding it difficult to let go. In such a case, you would like to learn how to analyze the person who hurt you in an attempt to understand why he hurt you. Then if you're able to understand the person better, you may find it easier to let that person go so you can move on with your life as a happier, more positive person.

Because of an Emotional Reaction

There are also some people who choose to learn this skill as a result of an emotional reaction. Sometimes, they don't even know that this emotional reaction caused them to start analyzing the other person. Emotions can be a powerful driving force and they can cause you to respond in different ways. You may start analyzing other people because you feel fixated on them. If this is your reason, tread lightly. Make sure that your reason behind wanting to analyze a specific person won't cause harm to you or to the person in question. For instance, if you're trying to analyze a person better in order for you to get closure and move on, that's okay. But if you feel like you're already becoming obsessed with the other person, you might want to find other people to focus on.

Avoidance

This may also be your reason for wanting to learn how to read people, especially if you have been hurt by someone in the past.

You may want to be able to see the "warning signs" early on so you don't have to deal with certain kinds of people. If this is your reason, you might also want to remember that people aren't always what they seem. You might have analyzed a person and judged him based on your analysis only to find out that your initial perception of the person wasn't entirely accurate. So you may use this skill to get a better understanding of another person, but it's also a good idea to give others the benefit of the doubt.

Thinking of Examples

Having this skill can be very useful in different situations. If someone asks you for advice, you can use this skill to give examples of why people may have acted the way they did. You can use the skill to help others understand their situations or the people in their lives. If you're in the habit of helping other people deal with their issues, then learning how to analyze others can be very beneficial for you. The more you understand other people, the more you will be able to guide others, too.

Chapter 3:
The Benefits of Analyzing People

Why is there a need for you to learn how to analyze others? Academically speaking, it's very interesting to acquire this skill because it will allow you to better understand those around you. But when you look at how this skill will affect your life, you'll realize how beneficial analyzing people can be. Try to think of it this way—the more you can understand yourself and the people around you, the more you will become successful in dealing with them and with the situations you find yourself in. Aside from this, there are other benefits that come with learning how to read people, including:

It Helps You Know More About Your Own Preferences

As individuals, we all have our own preferences. But do you really know your preferences, or do these change depending on the situation or on the people around you? The fact is, we all have these psychological type preferences. However, when other people - especially those who we admire or those who we want to impress - don't have the same preferences, we may end up changing ours. Sadly, this isn't beneficial for us.

When you operate within your own preferences, this brings out your most comfortable, effective, and efficient self. One of the best ways to do this is by learning how to analyze people. The more you get to know other people and understand them on a deeper level, the more you will come to realize the types of people or personalities you prefer. In other words, analyzing others also helps you analyze yourself.

Whenever you meet new people, you can already gauge whether you will get along with this person or not. Although first impressions aren't always reliable, you can use this skill to determine the best way to deal with the person. From there, you can start getting to know the person better to find out more about who he/she is and what makes him/her tick.

It Helps You with Your Career

In the conflict-avoiding benefit of analyzing people, we had explained how this skill can be beneficial at work. But it doesn't end there. Being able to effectively analyze others helps you with your career in other ways, too. For one, when you're being interviewed for a position, you may want to learn as much as you can about the interviewer. The more you learn about the interviewer, the more you will be able to analyze him/her. Then you will have a better idea of how to handle the interview in order to get the job.

The same thing goes for when you are the interviewer. All interviewers would like to find people who are a perfect fit for the vacant position. As you speak to the applicants, you should analyze them as well. There are certain things to look out for (which we will be discussing later on) that can help you scrutinize the potential candidates beyond what they say during the interview.

Also, learning how to analyze others—whether it be your boss, colleagues or subordinates—helps you deal with them more effectively. This skill enables you to communicate well with others and interact with them in the best possible way. Over time, your coworkers will start seeing you as an open-minded, approachable person who is able to get along well with different kinds of people.

It Helps You Appreciate Differences

Have you ever wondered why some people get along well with others while some people don't? This is because we are all different from one another. And while some people are able to build relationships with people of varying personalities, there are those who just can't seem to get along with certain types of individuals. This is a fact of life that we cannot escape from.

As you learn how to analyze people, you would also discover how their personality types differ from one another. There are certain personality types which mesh well with each other and there are those which, when combined, are like fire and ice. Analyzing others also allows you to recognize your own personality type and how different you are from those around you. As you discover the differences between individuals, you may also come to appreciate those differences. This is especially true when you're faced with situations which make you feel weak.

In such cases, you can ask other people to help you out—those who you know can handle the situation more effectively because they are your exact opposite. As you practice this skill, you will end up discovering different kinds of people, why they have these personalities, and how you can work with your differences in order to build stronger relationships.

It Helps with Your Empathy and Emotional Regulation

This skill also helps you become more empathic. The more you understand other people and what they are going through, the more you can hone your empathic accuracy skills. Imagine meeting someone new on one of your bad days, one of those days when you feel like everything is going wrong and you just can't handle the pressure of trying to impress others. How would you feel if the person you met judged you based on that first meeting? This person would think of you as aloof, snobbish, or even mean.

Now try to place yourself on the other side of the situation. Imagine meeting someone who is having a bad day. Chances are, your first impression of this person won't be a good one. But if you try to dig deeper, you'll find out that the person just acted that way because he was having a bad day. This is where empathy comes in. You will try to place yourself in the other person's situation in order to understand how he/she feels. The next time you meet or interact with this person, it would be like starting all over again.

Learning how to analyze people also helps with emotional regulation. The process of analyzing others helps you analyze your own emotions and how you react to people and situations. You'll be able to see things from the perspective of others which, in turn, helps you control your own emotions before you let them out.

It Helps You be More Sensitive Towards Other People

It's always easier to judge other people based on the things they say or the behaviors that they show. But just because it's easy, this doesn't make it right. Often, people act the way they do because they're going through something difficult or they've been through devastating situations in the past and these behaviors are part of their defense mechanism. Before you judge others, try analyzing them first in order to understand them better.

With this skill in your arsenal, you can start becoming more sensitive towards other people and their situations. Instead of judging a person based on what they did or said the first time you met them, it's more beneficial for both of you when you try getting to know them first. Once you understand what drives the actions or language of a person, you'll stop being so judgmental. Whether at work or in your personal life, being more sensitive towards others can go a long way.

This is especially true for when you meet people who are dealing with their own issues and who need support but are too afraid to ask for it. In such situations, you will be able to extend a helping hand willingly to make the other person feel that he/she isn't alone in the fight.

It Helps You Get to Know Others Better

Knowing how to analyze people effectively also helps you get to know them better and in a more profound way. Analyzing others involves learning about the culture of others and how they grew up to be the people they are now. To get this information, you have to dig a little deeper.

The bottom line is that this skill helps you break through the superficial layer in order to build a stronger foundation for your relationships. Even if you don't end up being friends with everyone you meet, learning more about them will help you interact more effectively. That way, no matter where you go and what types of people you meet, you'll feel more confident with your socialization skills.

It Helps You Avoid Conflicts

Learning how to analyze others can also help you prevent conflicts from happening. Part of learning this skill is learning about different personality types. In learning this, you would have a good idea of what might trigger other people which, in turn, makes them upset. For instance, through your analysis, you have determined that the person you're talking to tends to react negatively to loud, outspoken people. With this information, you can modify your behavior in order to avoid conflict.

You can even use your skill of being able to analyze people to help others become more receptive to their current situation. When people feel upset or angry about their situation, they tend to shut down or start arguments with others. This kind of reaction doesn't help improve the situation. Therefore, being able to avoid conflicts even before they arise will help you out immensely. In particular, this benefit is very significant when dealing with employees or colleagues. Conflicts tend to decrease productivity in the workplace, especially when they escalate. But if you're able to help diffuse the situation before it heats up, you can maintain the peace.

It Helps You Interpret What Others are Saying

Finally, although verbal communication is very effective, there are certain non-verbal cues which can help you better interpret what other people are saying. There are people who tend to speak indirectly and in order for you to understand them, you need to infer the meaning of their words. When dealing with such people directly, this could lead to misinterpretation which might eventually lead to conflict.

Conversing with other people while analyzing them is much more effective. Here, you are able to interpret the things you hear as well as the things you observe from the person you're talking to. This is especially beneficial when speaking to people whom you know very well. Over time, you will start learning more about how others speak and whether or not they mean what they are saying. Even for the people you've just met, analyzing them while speaking to them gives you a deeper interpretation of the messages they're trying to convey.

Chapter 4:
Things to Keep in Mind

Learning how to analyze people isn't an easy thing to do. This is a skill which involves a lot of practice. But the more you learn about it and the more you practice it, the better you will become at it. Now that you're reading this book, you probably have your own reasons for wanting to learn how to analyze other people. We've gone through the different benefits of having this skill and you can see that it can help you in different ways. But before you start studying those around you, there are things you must keep in mind first.

There are many things you must first learn before you can go out into the world and start practicing the skill. All of this information will help you understand the skill so that you will be able to apply it effectively.

The Person's Culture

Culture refers to the social or non-biological aspects of our lives. Anything we learn as we grow up in our own community is part of our culture. It's more than just our behaviors, it also includes our beliefs, values, norms, and even expressive symbols. Whenever you meet someone new, remember that this person may have a different culture than yours. Even if the person comes from the same country, he/she may have a culture that varies greatly from your own. This is why it's also important to consider a person's culture while analyzing.

Different countries have different cultures. But even within a large cultural group, there may be co-cultures and subcultures existing within that group. For instance, in Asian countries, the people who live there have certain cultures. But within each country, they have their own cultures and cultural practices too. And within those smaller cultures, there are even smaller subcultures which affect the beliefs, values, and norms of the people. As with all differences, it's important to accept and celebrate these different cultures. This will help you become more effective at analyzing others and interacting with people of varying backgrounds and cultures.

The Person's Gender

From the moment we are born, most of us are conditioned to differentiate women and men, femininity and masculinity. When you analyze people, you must consider their gender as well. Although this distinction may have been easier to make in the past, these days, we also have to consider (and be more considerate towards) the other genders - the LGBTQ community. In most countries, gender is no longer binary. Keep this in mind when you meet new people.

When taking this factor into consideration, you may want to be as open-minded as possible. If you believe in genderism—the cultural belief that there should only be two genders—you might find it challenging to truly analyze people who belong to the

LGBTQ community. This is a reality in our society now and with its acceptance, more and more people are finding the courage to speak up about their true gender. These days, it's not uncommon to meet people who are openly gay, bisexual, or transgender. When you meet such people, it's best to accept their life choices because there's really nothing you can do about it, especially when you've only met these people for the first time.

The Person's Age

The first thing you must consider when analyzing others is their age. Trying to analyze the behaviors of a child would vary greatly from when you're trying to analyze a teenager or an adult. Age is a very important factor to consider when studying others. People of the same age, those who grew up together, belong to "cultural generations." Often, these individuals share the same or similar experiences with other individuals of the same generation. Therefore, they usually have the same set of shared attitudes, values, and beliefs which differ from those who belong to other cultural generations. So when you're trying to analyze people from different cultural generations, consider the following variables:

- **Language**

    It's easier to differentiate generations by the way they use language. There is such a thing called a "generation gap" wherein different generations find it challenging to communicate with each other at times. When analyzing a person, you would have a better idea of which generation he/she is from by the language he/she uses. To give you a more concrete grasp of this, you may try watching films made in the past century or so and compare them with modern films. Right away, you will be able to see (or hear) the differences in how people use language.

- **Use of slang**

    Slang refers to a set of conversational terms and phrases which constantly change with the times. These are used by individuals to reinforce or establish their social cohesiveness or identity within society. Just like language, people of different ages use different slang when they communicate with each other. Right now, the most prominent users of these terms and phrases are the millennials, who have created a wide range of slang for their everyday conversations. If you really want to become a master of analyzing people, learning this slang will help you out a lot, especially when you deal with people of varying age groups.

- **Technological impact**

    Finally, the effect of technology can also be seen in people of different generations. Although language and slang can be adapted by varying generations, the development of technology has widened the gap between the younger and older generations. Keeping up with the times is another huge part of being able to analyze others and this includes learning all about the technological advancements which have an effect on the new generation.

The Person's Education

Not everyone you meet will have the same educational level as you. If you are lucky enough to hold a college degree or higher, don't assume that all the people you interact with, even those you meet in the corporate setting, have the same level of education as you. There may be times when you meet individuals who hold high positions in a company but who don't even hold a college degree. Such people are admirable because they must have reached their position through hard work and dedication. This shows that a person's educational level doesn't necessarily dictate their standing in life.

Conversely, you may also meet people who have achieved a high level of education but don't act like it. They may hold a bachelor's degree, a doctorate, or some other type of degree but their words and actions don't show it. The point here is that, although the education level is a factor, it isn't a surefire way to determine an individual's personality. Still, it's worth considering, especially when you're trying to analyze a person's academic aspect. You may ask questions about a person's education in order to find out more about his/her beliefs, values, and the things he/she stands for.

The Person's Occupation

Finally, the occupation of a person should also be taken into consideration upon analysis. Most people select their occupations based on interest and motivation. And the longer they stay in this chosen occupation, the more it will influence their behaviors and perceptions. This is why there are stereotypes about certain occupations. For instance, when you find out that someone is a teacher, you immediately think that this person is organized, methodical, and tends to be serious. Though this may be true for a lot of teachers, these characteristics won't apply to all of them.

Just like the other factors we have discussed, it's important to take them into consideration when analyzing people, but you shouldn't use these factors to make judgments. The more you find out about a person, the more you will be able to connect all of these factors to that person in order to see him/her as a whole person. Simply taking one factor into consideration then judging the person based on that factor won't make your analysis of the person effective. Instead, it's better to take all of these variables together and use them to make a more accurate analysis.

Chapter 5:
The Basics

Each time you meet a new person, how long do you need to make a first impression?

For most people, they would claim that upon meeting a new person, it takes them less than a minute to come up with a first impression. But according to studies, it actually takes a lot less time for people to make that all-important first impression. Psychologists have discovered that people only need a tenth of a second to develop a first impression of a new person and they mainly base this on their body language.

But what happens after you get that first impression?

If you maintain communication with the person, this is the perfect time to start analyzing him/her. And the longer you converse with the person, the easier it is to come up with a more accurate analysis. In this article, we will be starting with the basics of analyzing people. For any skill you need to learn, you should always start with the basics in order to get a better understanding of the concepts behind the skill. With that being said, let's begin.

The Rules of Understanding Others

Although there are some rules to follow when you're trying to analyze and understand other people, keep in mind that rules—no matter how many there are - can't define human behaviors as these are extremely complex. Still, these rules can help make your analysis of others easier and more effective. While you analyze other people, consider these guidelines:

- **Emotions are extremely important to most people**

    Always remember that people may feel stronger emotions about certain things than they let on. They just don't show these emotions because society tends to frown upon people who have regular outbursts of enthusiasm, happiness, depression, anger, and other flamboyant emotions. Therefore, as you try analyzing others, never assume that other people are perfectly fine just because they are handling the stresses of their lives well. Never call others out if they try to deceive others—this might just be their attempt at keeping their emotions under control.

    Try to be more sensitive or empathic towards others. If you feel like someone is going through a big issue and he/she is struggling with it, you can try probing a bit. Showing others that you accept their emotions instead of judging them makes it easier for them to open up to you and share what they are really thinking or feeling. When this happens, you will be able to understand them better and maybe even help them with the issue they're dealing with.

- **Keep in mind that there are very few explicit social behaviors**

    Simply put, this means that for most people, they conceal the intentions behind their behaviors. For instance, if a person feels angry or depressed, his/her behaviors upon meeting you won't show this. Think about it—when you're feeling highly emotional and you meet someone new, do you show your true emotions to that person? Chances are, you don't. Instead, you would put on a brave face to show common courtesy to the one you are meeting for the first time.

    So when you're meeting other people and you want to practice your analyzing skills, empathy should also come into play. Focus on the message behind the other person's words instead of just hearing them. This helps you build a genuine rapport with the person, especially if you learn the art of appropriate probing. When you focus on empathizing with other people, you will be able to break down any subversion allowing you to get to the very heart of the issue.

- **Never assume malice in other people**

    It's never a good idea to always assume that people care about you or they are showing malice towards you - no matter how they act when you first meet them. Generally, when people meet others, most thoughts that run through their minds are self-directed. Some thoughts are focused on relationships, mainly on how these relationships affect them. Finally, there are very few thoughts which are focused on empathy wherein the person tries to see the perspective and feel the emotions of another person.

When someone meets you, this interaction would only take up a very small part of that person's mind. Unless the person had already seen you from far away and he/she really wants to meet you, chances are, the person doesn't have any preconceived notions about you. In fact, even if the person is thinking about you, it's more about how your interaction would affect him/her, not about you or who you are.

Therefore, when you meet other people and practice your skill of analyzing others, don't put any malice into your assessment either. Be as objective as you possibly can so that you don't come up with an analysis that's biased or subjective.

- **People focus too much on themselves sometimes**

This may sound selfish, but it is true. When people hear this fact, they might raise their eyebrows at the very thought of it. But when they try to analyze themselves, they would come to realize that being self-absorbed is something we all suffer from. This doesn't necessarily have to be a bad thing. For instance, if you focus on yourself for the purpose of self-improvement, then that's a good thing.

But when you're done improving yourself and dealing with your own issues, it would be better for you to start focusing on other people as well. Being able to go beyond yourself allows you to be able to analyze and understand others more profoundly. Don't get hung up on yourself all the time. Give other people your attention too. That way, they may learn from your example and start opening up to others as well.

- **Selfish altruism usually dictates a person's behavior**

    This is an important point to keep in mind. As much as we don't want to admit it, most of us are driven by selfish altruism. This is when a person shows a good impression or does good things because it helps themselves either directly or indirectly. For instance, if you are in a position of power, you may notice that a lot of people smile broadly and treat you with the utmost respect when meeting you for the first time.

    But if you are just "one of the crowd," people might not show as much enthusiasm when they are being introduced to you. You don't have to feel bad about this—it's just how people are! When it comes to selfish altruism and behaviors, there are certain situations where this characteristic is more evident. These include:

    - **When dealing with family**

        People tend to treat members of their family differently than they would treat other people—sometimes, this even extends to relatives and close friends. This is just how we are designed, and it also shows self-altruism as you know that the people closest to you would treat you the same way in similar situations.

- **When implied reciprocity exists**

   A lot of people base their behaviors on the idea that if they help others, those people will help them in return. Again, this is a very common way of thinking. But if you are able to identify these kinds of people, you will have a better understanding of why they behave the way they do.

- **When trying to achieve status**

   When you treat others well and offer to help them, this can be seen as a sign of power. Upon meeting new people, offering help, advice or assistance shows others that you are approachable and capable. When you try to analyze others, you can try to determine whether they are genuinely trying to help or they are offering their services just to achieve status. This helps you learn how to deal with others better.

- **When making transactions/purchases**

   If you're looking to purchase something, both you and the salesperson you talk to would benefit from your transaction. Therefore, you would treat each other well. Through the transaction, you are able to purchase what you are looking for and the salesperson would be able to make a sale. This is even more beneficial for the salesperson if he/she earns income from commissions. So you would be nice to each other even if you don't have any emotional bond because this would be beneficial to both of you.

- **A lot of people feel lonely—even if they don't want to admit it**

    Even though some people seem to have it all, deep down, they may feel lonely. As human beings, we are social animals. But we are also focused on other things like earning a lot of money, becoming famous, or trying to make a difference in the world. We don't spend enough time investing in relationships and yet we are afraid of becoming ostracized.

    Being aware of this fact helps you understand that being lonely is a common thing. Even when you feel lonely, you should know that other people feel this too. So what should you do about this? The best thing you can do is get out there and get to know other people better—really get to know them. While you practice analyzing others, you should also try to build your relationship with them. The more you do this, the more human interaction you will have. Making friends and building relationships make you less lonely, and it also combats the loneliness that is felt by those you build relationships with.

- **Most people have poor memories—especially in terms of meeting others**

    With the exception of those who have an excellent memory, most people have trouble remembering things— like the names or other details about new people they meet. This is especially true if they meet others in casual situations like at parties and other social gatherings. Of course, if you were introduced to someone important, you would definitely remember him/her.

It's easier for people to remember meeting others when they are introduced in an interesting way or if, upon meeting, they discover that they share something in common. But if you want to be effective at analyzing others, you should try to improve your memory. That way, you can recall everyone you meet and when you meet them again, you can "pick up where you left off." It's important to keep this rule in mind so you don't end up feeling bad when other people don't remember meeting you. As long as you remember your first encounter, you will be able to use your memory to start analyzing the other person as you interact with him/her more.

The Different Personality Types

One thing you have to consider—and accept—when analyzing others is that people have different personality types. It's important to realize that people use different aspects of their personalities throughout the day. Therefore, as you analyze, keep this in mind so you don't end up making premature analyses of others based on the first aspect of their personality you have seen or experienced. It would also be very useful for you to learn about the different personality types to help you determine the personality types of those you meet. This can also help you improve relationships, communicate effectively, exert your influence, and be successful in your efforts to learn more about others.

There are so many different types of personalities out there, and learning all of them would be a huge achievement. But even if you're able to learn and understand these personality types, applying your knowledge to the analysis of people is another thing. To help you practice, you may want to analyze your own personality first. When it comes to analyzing your personality, there are two main aspects to think about: first, how your personalities work and second, how you can apply these to your life. When you are able to do this, you will find it easier to start analyzing the personalities of others and use this to interact with them more effectively. Here are some of the most common personality types and short descriptions of them:

- **Introverted Feeling**

    People with this personality type listen intently. They focus on your tone of voice, your motivations, the words that show your values, and even what is left unsaid. Therefore, you must speak to them thoughtfully. When you work with such people, take the time to think about what you want to say. After they listen to your words, you might be surprised at how definitive they are when it comes to decision-making. Speak to their values, especially the ones which are positive. Just make sure that you stay true to yourself no matter what.

- **Extroverted Feeling**

    People with this personality type pay close attention to what you say and how you evaluate them—but they don't show it in an outward way. The ethical value of the triumphs, failures, and choices of others is very important to them, therefore, it's best to give them a chance to discuss injustice and justice considerations. When you work with such people, make use of and respond to language that is heavy with value and meaning. Focus on your choice of words instead of your tone of voice.

- **Introverted Intuiting**

    People with this personality type don't do well with mundane demands and external stimulation. Eliminate these from the equation and they will be able to access their internal processes. When you work with such people, you must provide them with a sensory or physical focus. Also, give them time to explore their visions of the future so they can work on the specific steps for them to reach those visions.

- **Extroverted Intuiting**

    People with this personality type work more effectively during brainstorming when there are diverse inputs present. When you work with such people, don't be too strict when it comes to sensory distractions. Allow the person to get different inputs from different sources instead of forcing them to work in a linear way. Focus on ideas, meanings, analogies, and more. Wordplay, humor, and other cognitive games may work well too.

- **Introverted Sensing**

    People with this personality type are most comfortable in low-key environments with minimal distractions. This gives them a chance to focus on their experiences and review the situation so they can learn. When you work with such people, provide step-by-step methodologies so they can develop their skills. This also gives them a "road map" so they can keep track of their progress and prioritize tasks more effectively. When you need to provide feedback, be as sensitive as possible even to your non-verbal cues.

- **Extroverted Sensing**

    People with this personality type are most comfortable in stimulating environments that are rich in sensory inputs. These include places with enticing scenery, interesting decor, and a lot of windows. When you work with such people, encourage them to move, focus on achievable challenges, and allow for resourceful responses.

- **Introverted Thinking**

    People with this personality type depend more on complex and sophisticated reasoning and they use multiple methods such as weighing odds, categorizing, deducing, and the like. The thought processes of these people aren't directly related to sensory inputs, therefore, when they make decisions, these are usually detached and deep. When you work with such people, give them time to clarify their work as they tend to make a lot of mistakes—which they correct on their own. Such people strive for accuracy before they implement their plans. Therefore, it's recommended to provide them with ways to address excessive emotional and social data as these tend to overwhelm them.

- **Extroverted Thinking**

    People with this personality type utilize their brains in a way that is energy-efficient. They depend on measurable elements, decision-making, and hearing words. When you work with such people, present information in the form of figures and facts or in the form of visual formats such as grids, charts, and diagrams. Just be careful not to mistake their speed and confidence for competence.

Learning about the different personality types and exploring how you can relate to them allows you to realize the value of others and listen to what they really have to say. This makes you more effective at communicating with them and analyzing them, too.

One word of caution—the study of personality isn't a closed book. Although these personality types may help guide you, be open to the fact that you might encounter people who don't fall into these personality types. Or, there may be people who display characteristics of more than just one of these personality types. Even if you read other books and articles, you may come across other information about personality types and how to deal with them.

The more you learn about all of this, the clearer personality becomes. However, studies and research are still ongoing. Human behavior experts are still discovering more about personality and the different changes these undergo because of factors such as time, culture, gender, and so on. The bottom line is to always keep an open mind when dealing with people. This makes everything easier for you and for the people around you.

Learning How to Profile People

In order to analyze people effectively, you must learn how to understand their psychology, and you can do this by learning how to profile people. To prepare yourself to learn this skill, take a moment to pause and watch others. While most people are focused on their goals—or getting from point A to point B—you must learn how to pay attention to others and notice all the details. In other words, you should learn how to see beyond what other people see. Here are some steps to help you learn profiling:

- **Get down to the basics**

    People are like onions. They have layers and the more you discover these layers, the more you will be able to read the person. Let's have an example to illustrate this analogy:

    - The skin of an onion is the first layer—for people, this layer shows the traits and personalities people have towards others.
    - You can get to the next layer by getting to know the person better. This allows you to establish the foundation of your relationship while being able to understand them better.
    - The next layer is uncovered when you have already established trust with the other person. By the time you reach this layer, you are able to connect personally with the other person. You may share secrets, fears, worries, and other sensitive information at this point.
    - Although you can continue analyzing others to discover more about them, you probably won't go

into the person's "core." This is because the core is where secrets and thoughts aren't shared with others. This is more of a psychological layer that people can only discover within themselves.

When you're trying to profile a person, you should consciously remove any projection barriers you may have. This means that you should accept the truth of the person and the situation instead of forcing yourself to believe otherwise. Also, you must work on eliminating prejudice when profiling others. Prejudice is a powerful barrier that prevents you from getting an accurate picture of the person you are trying to profile. Make sure that you are in a neutral state of mind before you start the process.

- **Find a person to practice on**

To practice profiling, start by finding a test subject—preferably someone you already know. You may profile strangers, but this would take more time. Since you will just be practicing, profiling someone you know is easier. Once you have your test subject, follow these steps:

  ○ Determine the person's baseline profile—this is their rest state or comfort zone. Randomly observe the person at different times of the day. Take note of how they react to situations, assess them at different times and days, and observe their interactions with others.
  ○ Review the notes you have taken to determine patterns of behavior. These patterns help you build the foundation so you can start knowing what is true—and what is not—about the person.

- Next, focus on non-patterns. These include the unexpected behaviors or reactions of the person that don't fit into the baseline profile.

- **Learn more...**

    Now that you have the baseline profile of your test subject, it's time to learn more about them. This is where you define who the person is, allowing their styles, appearance, and personal being to become "them" as a person. Recognize how your test subject vocalizes. Soft tones indicate that the person is shy, while loud tones indicate that the person may have the need to take command or feel higher compared to other people.

    Also, learn how to differentiate between slang, exaggerations, sarcasm, and other types of verbal expressions typically used in conversations. Listening to the contextual flow of words helps you determine if the person has a good background in terms of education or they are just trying to sound smarter than they actually are.

    The next thing to do is analyze your test subject's personal space. Do this by relating their work or home life to how they present themselves to the public. See the type of neighborhood they live in and their organizational skills at home or at work. Most people who have busy schedules might not be able to keep their surroundings as tidy as they would like to. Don't assume that just because their surroundings aren't organized, it means that they are lazy. Usually, though, most people who are very organized—even in their surroundings—are also very confident. They seldom feel stressed no matter what the situation is.

Try to observe how your test subject shares their personal life with other people. While a lot of people don't feel secure or confident in the eyes of the public, they show their true selves when they are in their comfort zone. Observing how your test subject interacts with others will give you a lot of valuable information for your profile.

A person's appearance also says a lot about them. Review your test subject's fashion, and how they present themselves each day. Does the person dress casually all the time or do they always dress up in formal clothes? Review your test subject's hairstyle, too. Is the person's hair styled, or does it seem like they just brushed their hair enough to make it look okay? From head to toe, the appearance of a person says a lot about who they are. Other things to observe include:

- How they react to unexpected occurrences in public such as when they sneeze, burp, cough, and more. This shows you how much basic etiquette the person knows.
- The person's eye movements. Do they look right at you when you talk or do they stare at something else? Try to observe the paths their eyes go when you detect lies.
- Assess the person's self-composure while around other people. Some people become nervous when there are many people around, while others thrive on social interaction.
- Also, try to observe for any signs of nervousness or impatience such as tapping their feet, fidgeting, sighing, lip biting, and more.

Basically, profiling involves a lot of observation and learning. Don't expect to be an expert profiler from the get-go. This is a skill that you need to practice. The more you practice it, the more efficient you become at it.

Chapter 6:
Some of the Best Methods for Analyzing People

When it comes to analyzing people, there are different methods and approaches for you to do this. Learning these methods will help you determine the best way to analyze each person you meet. You can also use the different methods based on the situation and on the people that you encounter in your life. Of course, you should also remember that your initial analysis of a person may change the more you get to know them.

Your first impression of a person is important—but it shouldn't be your only basis for your analysis. If you really want to learn everything about a person, this takes a lot of time, effort, and communications. However, the methods you will learn in this chapter will surely go a long way in helping you analyze people successfully.

What Our Faces Say About Us

Simple as this method may seem, it can be very effective when you do it properly. Analyzing the personality of a person by looking at their face is known as "facial profiling." Using this method to know and understand others is useful for improving your communication and making the best possible decisions about the people you interact with. Your face reveals your personality, and with the growing popularity of social media platforms, facial profiling has become a lot easier.

When you learn how to accurately read faces, this can help improve your communication with others from your first impression of them. Faces can be used as a predictor of behaviors and personality. According to studies, our genes can affect our personalities—and since our faces reflect our DNA, they can also reflect our personality. Genes play an important role in the determination of our fundamental personality traits such as learning and social skills. Aside from the genetic factor, the other important aspects of facial profiling you should learn are:

- **Facial gestures**

    These can provide you with a wealth of information about the motivations, feelings, and thoughts of a person. If you want to successfully analyze the faces of people, observe the following:

    - The movement of the person's lips and tongue.
    - The various types of frowns and smiles the person uses.
    - Blinking patterns and eye movements of the person.
    - Whether the person squints their eyes or not.
    - Whether the person maintains eye contact or looks at a different point while conversing with you.
    - Movements of the person's eyebrows.
    - Any tension in the person's facial muscles.

- Wrinkling of the person's forehead, nose, and more.

Observing each of these facial signals may help you unlock the various aspects of a person. Just make sure that you pay attention to the movement patterns of the person's face along with the factors that trigger these movements.

- **Constriction or dilation of the pupils**

Learning how to identify the variations in a person's pupils can also help you with your facial profiling. When you see that the person's pupils are large or dilated, this indicates that they are feeling relaxed, they're enjoying the conversation, or they are openly accepting your ideas. In some cases, dilated pupils may also indicate that the person is in love with you. Conversely, when you see that the person's pupils are small or constricted, this indicates that they don't trust you, they don't believe you, or they don't agree with your ideas.

One thing to remember when it comes to the constriction or dilation of the pupils is that this can be influenced by the lighting in your environment and the other person's health or state of mind. Therefore, you should only use your observation of the person's pupils along with the other facial cues to come up with an accurate analysis.

- **Becoming pale or blushing**

As you are talking with another person, you may observe changes in the colors of their faces or how intense their skin-tone is. You may say some things that have a profound effect on the other person's emotional level. Although they may not express their thoughts and feelings verbally to you, the change in the color of their face is something they cannot hide.

Unless a person is suffering from any kind of medical condition, when they turn pale, this may indicate that they are either shocked or fearful of what you just said. But if the person starts blushing, this may be an indication of anger, embarrassment or disagreement with you. When observing this aspect of a person's face, consider the context of your situation so you can come up with a more precise interpretation.

Analyzing Others on Sight

Another method of analyzing other people is by analyzing on sight. While this isn't the most accurate way to analyze others, you can use this to have a baseline or foundation to use for your future observations. There are five main types of people and you can classify them based on their physical appearance. The first thing that happens when you meet new people is you see their physique. Apart from their face, you would look at the person from head to toe—and through this simple gesture, you can already come up with a simple analysis.

1. **Thinker or Cerebral Type**

   These people may have frail bodies because they focus more on developing their minds. They are imaginative dreamers who are good at visualization and meditation. In terms of personality, they tend to be more serious compared to other personality types. Once they start talking about a topic, they tend to go in-depth during the discussion. Also, they tend to lack the social skills required to build good relationships with others.

2. Enjoyer or Alimentative Type

These people are overweight, obese, or fat. For men, they are wide around the girth and for women, they are wide around the hips. In terms of personality, such people usually find comfort in food and they enjoy tasting different kinds of food. They have excellent social skills and family is extremely important to them.

3. Worker or Muscular Type

Obviously, these people have a large, muscular build that makes them stand out in crowds. They are more action-oriented than intellectual and they tend to lead very active lifestyles. In terms of personality, such people are doers. They focus on action and execution instead of planning and organization.

4. Thriller or Thoracic Type

These people hold their chests up high and are florid-faced. Since they have large chests, they are able to breathe easily, making them more relaxed. In terms of personality, such people may hold high positions of power or may have a lot of accomplishments. When you get into an argument with this type of person, they won't stay mad at you for long. They are smart, admirable, and they tend to have a good sense of style.

5. **Stayer or Osseous Type**

   These people have a bony framework that is highly developed compared to other types of people. They are lean and are probably the most health-conscious types of people. In terms of personality, such people are reliable and firm. Despite having a somewhat stoic nature, they are very responsible and punctual. However, they aren't that open to change as even their thinking is very firm.

These are simple, generalized descriptions based on the physical appearances of people. You may consider these while analyzing others and try to see if these personalities are, indeed, true for people with these physiques. Of course, there are always exceptions to the rules. The more you learn how to analyze people—and all of their aspects—the more effectively you will be able to come up with a good analysis of another person on sight.

Some Awesome Secrets Shared by Experts

Your ability to analyze others will have a significant effect on how you deal and communicate with them. The more you are able to understand others along with their thoughts and feelings, the more you can adjust your communication style and the message you want to convey so that the other person receives it in the best possible way. After analyzing the faces and physiques of the people you meet and you come up with your initial analysis, it's time to dig deeper. Here are some tips for analyzing others as shared by experts:

- **Come up with a baseline**

    All people come with their own quirks and behavior patterns. For instance, during conversations, some people may keep their arms crossed, clear their throat frequently, fix their hair, pout, squint, or do other actions. Unless you are consciously trying to analyze others, you might not even notice these things. Even if you do notice them, you won't really give these actions much thought.

    But if you want to gain the skill of analyzing others, don't just dismiss these behaviors. The fact is, people have varying reasons for doing these things. They may be simple mannerisms, but in some cases, these actions may indicate nervousness, anger, deception, or other strong emotions. When you observe these things, try to come up with a mental baseline of the "normal behaviors" of other people. Doing this aids in your analysis the more you get to know others.

- **Search for deviations and differences**

    Once you have your mental baseline, it's time to bring out your observation skills. Try to search for deviations, differences, or inconsistencies shown by the other person based on the baseline you have created. For instance, if you are dealing with a supplier at work and you noticed that when he/she is nervous, he/she tends to scratch his/her forehead frequently.

    When this supplier tries to make some changes to your agreed-upon contract, you notice these behaviors. As such, you may want to probe further by asking questions to the supplier. That way, you can find out the real reason for the changes they are suggesting. Noticing these deviations gives you an edge, especially over people who are trying to gain the upper hand or those who are trying to trick you into agreeing with them.

- **Observe gesture clusters**

    While no single word or gesture would necessarily mean something, when you observe clusters of gestures, it's time to pay more attention. Going back to our example, you may notice that aside from the forehead scratching, the supplier's eyes are also darting around nervously as he/she shifts his/her weight from one foot to another. As these gestures are being done together, this may indicate that the person is trying to finish the conversation as soon as possible. In such a situation, proceed cautiously.

- **Observe the person's walk**

    You can easily identify people who lack self-confidence by the way they walk. Often, such people shuffle along with their heads hung low and their movements lack flowing motions. Conversely, confident people walk with confidence—their heads held up high, chest out, and they walk with a purpose.

    Learning to analyze how other people work can help in different ways. For instance, when you have a team member who has a walk that indicates low confidence, you can take the necessary steps to help them out. You can help build your team member's confidence which, in turn, improves your team as a whole.

- **Make comparisons**

    Once you have noticed that the person you are talking to is acting unusual, the next step is to compare. Try to notice if the person acts the same way or displays the same behaviors with other people. After your conversation, you can step back and casually walk away. As you do this, try to inconspicuously observe the person as he/she starts conversations with others. Compare the person's expressions, tone of voice, body language, and posture with how he/she interacted or communicated with you.

- **Consider mirroring**

    Our brains have mirror neurons that cause us to reflect the state of mind of other people. This means that our brains are wired in such a way to allow us to read the body language of others. This means that when another person smiles at you, the tendency is that you would smile back. If the person frowns at you, it's likely that you would frown back.

    This tip can help you determine whether the person you are talking to feels happy or comfortable with you or not. You can try using mirroring to see if the other person will reciprocate your behaviors. If not, he/she may not like you, may not agree with you, or may feel unhappy because of something you have said or done.

- **Learn to identify the person with a "strong voice"**

    Just because a person occupies a seat of power, this doesn't mean that he/she is the most powerful person in the room.

Try to observe who has the "strong voice" as this person is usually the most confident—and usually, the most powerful. Such people would also have an expansive posture and a big smile on their face.

When you're sharing your ideas with other people, the tendency would be to give the leader of the group the most attention. However, if the leader has a weak or timid personality, your idea might not get approved. Instead, identify the person with a strong voice and focus more on him/her. Usually, groups—even leaders—turn to these people when it's time to make decisions. If you are able to convince that person, you can increase your likelihood of success.

- **Learn how to identify action words**

    Most of the time, the easiest and most effective way to get into the head of another person is through words. Since words are representations of thoughts, learning how to identify action words will help you understand meanings more effectively.

    For instance, when you have pitched an idea at work and when you ask for an update, they tell you that they "decided to go with another person's suggestion." In this sentence, the action word here is "decided." This word indicates that the people who made the decision aren't impulsive, they weighed the options carefully, and thought things through. This is a lot better than when you are simply told something like "wanted to go a different direction" as the word "wanted" comes with some subjectivity.

Action words give you valuable insights into how other people think. Therefore, learning how to identify them can help you analyze others better.

- **Look for clues**

    We all have our own unique personalities. But, there are some fundamental personality clues that may help you relate to other people, thus allowing you to read them more accurately. Here are some clues to look out for:

    - Does the person have a tendency to feed his/her ego?
    - Does the person appear to be driven by significance or by relationships?
    - Does the person tend to exhibit more extroverted or introverted behavior?
    - Does the person handle uncertainty and risk well or not?
    - How does the person behave when in relaxed environments?
    - How does the person behave when faced with stressful situations?

    Answering these questions as you analyze others can provide you with valuable clues about their personality.

Becoming skilled at analyzing others doesn't require you to be an expert investigator or interrogator. Using all these tips can help you figure out the thoughts and feelings of the people around you. As long as you know what to look for, you will be able to analyze others and get to know them in a more profound way.

Psychological Tricks to Help You Analyze People Easily

Have you ever wondered how different your life would be if you had the ability to read other people's minds? While some people have a strong sense of intuition that they use to get to know others better, some people aren't as perceptive. If you are one such person, the next thing you can do is "read" the body language of the people you interact with. It's a fact that you can get more than 55% of the information you need by tuning in to non-verbal communication. Observing another person's gestures, mimics, and other movements of their bodies would be like unmasking them so you can see their real feelings or thoughts. Consider these different body movements and what they mean so you can start observing others upon meeting or conversing with them:

- **When a person maintains eye contact**

    People who maintain eye contact while communicating are great at it. By maintaining eye contact, you are able to read all the emotions and feelings of the person you are talking to. It's also easier to analyze people who maintain eye contact because you can see their eyes and faces clearly.

- **When a person presents his/her face**

    In general, people do this as a means to attract the one they are speaking to. When people place their chin on their palm, they are presenting their faces and for you to see clearly. For men, this is the perfect time to give a compliment to the woman, especially if they find the woman attractive.

- **When a person fixes his/her appearance**

  As with presenting the face, this is another gesture people do when they are attracted to the one they're talking to. They try to make themselves look as presentable as possible and this indicates interest in the other party.

- **When a person plays with his/her shoe**

  When women do this, they might be trying to draw your attention to their legs. This gesture shows that women are relaxed and calm. In some cases, men may see this as a "green light."

- **When a person gives you a "glove handshake"**

  When a person shakes your hand and places his/her free hand on your wrist, they are trying to tell you that you can trust them.

- **When a person rubs his/her hands together**

  Experts believe that our hands show what our mind is thinking. So when you are talking to another person and they're rubbing their hands together, this may mean that they are feeling positive or hopeful about something. You may do this when thinking about possible benefits you can expect from the future.

- **When a person shakes your hand palm-down**

  This kind of handshake shows that you are ready and willing to help the other person.

- **When a person bites or nibbles at an object**

  Try to notice when the people you talk to are biting or nibbling at objects like pens or even the arms of their eyeglasses. When you see this behavior, try to cheer up or support the other person, as this indicated a feeling of worry. They may be nibbling at these objects as it makes them feel "safe."

- **When a person swings forward and back**

  This gesture may seem like something children would do, but some adults do it too. When a person does this, it may be an indication that they are feeling anxious.

- **When a person rubs his/her chin**

  Often, people do this when they need to make a choice or a decision. While rubbing their chin, they may be looking in different directions. In some cases, they might not even know exactly what they're looking at because they are lost in their thoughts.

- **When a person collects non-existent hairs**

  This is a type of "displacement gesture" that often indicates that the person disagrees with you, but is too polite to express his/her disagreement. Even though such people don't agree with what has been presented or said, they won't express their thoughts and opinions.

- **When a person keeps closing his/her eyes**

    When you are talking to another person and they close their eyes frequently, this may mean that they're trying to hide their true selves from the world. This action doesn't necessarily mean that the person is afraid of you. Instead, they may be doing this as an attempt to end the conversation. When they close their eyes, they won't be able to see you!

- **When a person covers his/her mouth with his/her hand**

    Back when you were still young, do you remember doing this when you didn't want to answer when your parents asked you a question? Well, some adults do this too. Sometimes, placing a palm, a couple of fingers or even the whole fist near the mouth helps some people restrain themselves from disclosing information. There are even cases where people try to disguise this gesture by pretending to cough.

- **When a person crosses his/her arms**

    This is a very common gesture that makes people comfortable. Unfortunately, it's also an indication that the person is shutting himself/herself off from others. People often cross their arms when they feel irritated. So if you are talking to someone and they cross their arms, you may want to ask why.

- **When a person leans forward**

  People would usually do this when they want you to make contact with them. Although their lower body may remain in the same position, they may lean their upper body forward almost intuitively.

- **When a person leans back**

  When, in the middle of your conversation, the person you're talking to leans back, this indicates that they are tired or "done" with your conversation. This may also indicate that a person doesn't feel comfortable with the one they are speaking to.

- **When a person shakes your hand palm-up**

  When a person shakes your hand this way, he/she may be showing sympathy towards you. But if you have been shaking hands for some time and the person shifts his/her hand this way, this may be a subtle way of telling you that he/she is in charge.

- **When a person shakes your hand and touches you**

  There are times when people shake hands with others then use their free hands to touch the other person's back, forearm, elbow or any other part of the body. For a lot of people, this feels like an invasion of space. And, it may indicate that the person lacks proper communication. The more "inappropriate" the touch is, the more the person needs to learn how to interact with others better.

- **When a person places his/her feet on the table**

    This gesture is one that raises eyebrows as it comes with a lot of negative connotations. It may express disrespect, bad manners, self-centeredness or the person is trying to show you who's the boss. If you find this position comfortable, don't do it in front of others!

- **When a person mounts a chair like a horse**

    For a lot of people, when someone they are talking to sits like this, they feel like it's a gesture of aggression. Therefore, it's no wonder that dominant people frequently take this position. If someone sits like this in front of you, stand up so you won't seem weak or dominated.

Chapter 7:
The Art of Analyzing Others

Analyzing other people is an art—it's not something you can learn overnight just by reading a book (even if that book is as informative and enriching as this one). One aspect of analyzing others is learning how to unlock certain psychological aspects to help you piece together human personality. This allows you to gain a deeper insight into the motives and thoughts of people no matter what they tell you verbally. It also helps you strengthen your influential and persuasive abilities in order to communicate more effectively with others. Let's start this chapter off with some tips to help you unlock these significant psychological aspects.

1. **Questions for identification**

   As you try to analyze the behaviors of another person, there are several questions you must ask yourself. These questions are crucial for you to develop as a more effective thinker. Also, the questions help you gather profound insights into the motives and meanings behind the most subtle cues people give away through their behaviors. You must continuously rotate these identification questions through your mind until you have gathered everything you need to unlock a person's "psychological recipe", thus allowing you to influence their thoughts. Some examples of these questions are:

- What do the cues mean?
- What do the cues reveal about the person?
- What is the significance of these cues?
- How can I change my approach in order to influence the other person?

2. Your ability to be psychologically perceptive

Throughout your interaction with other people, they will show you several categorized signals. You must learn how to catch these signals while communicating with others. Each of these signals has their own definite and specific meaning that, once understood, will reveal a wealth of information about the other person. As you unlock these signals, you will be able to think of more effective ways to win the other person over.

As you first try to be aware of these signals and analyze them, you may feel overwhelmed. This process requires a lot of conscious effort, meaningful questions, and thorough observation. Don't expect yourself to be able to catch all signals and cues from the start. Think of it as a journey of discovery. The more you practice, the more you will be to learn and improve.

Whenever you come in contact with another person, try to pay attention to the most obvious variables and signals. Over time, you will be able to catch these easily, therefore, you can focus more on the subtler signals. You know that you have become a master of observation when you are able to catch all the signals, cues, and variables people are giving off in a matter of minutes. After that, you can start digging deeper to find out the meanings of these signals and the answers to your questions. This, in turn, allows you to unlock what other people are consciously—or unconsciously—trying to hide.

3. Learning how to read emotional energy

Finally, you must also learn how to read other people's emotional energy. This is another skill that gets better with practice. But since it's even more abstract, you may have to practice a lot in order to become better. Here are some tips for you:

- Whenever you shake hands with another person, observe how it makes you feel. Does the handshake make you feel cold or warm? This simple action helps you evaluate another person's energy.
- Make eye contact with the other person—this is where you will see the person's emotional energy. There is truth to the old saying, "The eyes are the windows to the soul." Therefore, eye contact is essential.
- Instead of thinking too much about your interaction, try using your intuition. Does communicating with the other person feel good, or is there something off about your interaction? You should learn how to pay attention to your "gut feeling" about a person.
- Determine the energy type of the person. According to ancient thinkers, people have overall energy that can be described using the five

elements. When you understand these elements, you will be able to understand others better. These energy types are:

- People with water energy are often objective and peaceful.
- People with fire energy are often exciting, flamboyant, and sometimes hysterical.
- People with earth energy are often methodical and practical.
- People with wood energy are often new, energetic, and vital.
- People with metal energy are often withdrawn and depressed.

Keeping all of these things in mind can help you become more effective at analyzing others. Add this information to your existing knowledge along with everything else you have learned from this book thus far. But we are not done yet! There is still more to discover on your path towards learning the art of analyzing others.

Analyzing the Mind

Have you ever wished that you could understand someone else's mind? This would be such a cool skill or superpower to have. When you can read other people's minds, this will open you up to endless possibilities. However, since this isn't really possible, the next best thing would be to learn how to analyze the minds of others. This will help you guess what they are thinking about.

When it comes to analyzing the mind, the first thing you need to do is pay attention to the gestures of the person you are talking to.

Why?

Because these gestures are a reflection of what people are thinking about. Think about it—when you have something on your mind, do you always come out and say it? Chances are, you don't. After all, if one of your friends excitedly boasts about their new haircut which you hate, you won't really tell them that they don't look good, right? But when you start feeling or thinking something and you try to conceal it, you might unconsciously manifest these thoughts and feelings through your gestures. Remember the psychological tricks in the last chapter? You can go through those again and try to remember them as you interact with other people.

Apart from these gestures, you can also learn about the personality building blocks of people. In some cases, people manifest these building blocks consciously while others may manifest without them even knowing it. Take a look at these building blocks, as they can help you learn more about what is in the minds of other people:

1. **Attitude**

    Our attitudes are manifestations of our personalities. They remain the same no matter how much our external environment changes. When certain circumstances and events happen, pay close attention to how people react as this reveals their attitude along with other mysteries hidden in their minds.

2. **Behaviors**

    Gestures aren't the only things to watch out for when you are trying to analyze the minds of other people. The way people behave will tell you a lot about what they are thinking as well. When it comes to behaviors, they can be classified into:

- **Behaviors specific to the situation**

    These refer to the behaviors of people when they are faced with certain social situations. Seeing how other people deal with such situations will give you some unique insights into their emotional self-control and thinking patterns. Let's take a look at these behaviors:

    - **Communication style**

        Generally, you can classify people into three categories in terms of their communication style—Auditory, Kinesthetic, and Visual. As you observe other people, try to determine their communication style so you can adjust your own in order to match with theirs.

    - **Food and beverage consumption**

        Have you ever heard the saying, "We are what we eat?" Most of the time, this saying proves to be very accurate. You can get a lot of insights from the food and beverage consumption of people regarding their beliefs and values. You might even discover more profound insights into the underlying thought patterns and motives of others by analyzing something as simple as what they eat and drink.

Analyzing eating patterns is also helpful. For instance, you may notice that one person consumes small portions because they want to shed a couple of pounds. Then there are people who consume meals that are high in protein in order to gain more muscle. Through your observations, you have learned new things about others without even communicating with them. While these are generalized analyses of others, collecting all of this information will put you in a better position in terms of influencing their way of thinking.

- **Role model and peer influence**

Most of the time, people behave depending on how other people around them behave as well. Therefore, you should try to observe the actions, decisions, and even the subtlest movements of a person's face and body while they are interacting with their peers or role models. These will provide you with a lot of insights about the person and the manner by which they relate with others.

If you want to learn more about a person, try to find out who their role models are. These are the people they look up to for support, guidance, and inspiration. Knowing who their role models are will give you a better idea of a person's emotional life, values, thoughts, and beliefs.

- **Behaviors specific to social tendencies**

People tend to reveal their different aspects when faced with emotional and social situations. They behave the way they do because of their social tendencies. Therefore, you can't say that you really know a person—or that you have come up with a comprehensive analysis of a person until you've witnessed the following:

- **How a person behaves when alone**

    We all act differently when we think that nobody is watching. This is the time when people will reveal their true personalities. While with others, people tend to "put their best foot forward." This is because we all want to fit in, be liked by others, and feel appreciated. Therefore, people would behave and respond accordingly, even if it's something they don't really want to do.

- **How a person behaves when feeling relaxed**

    When people are most relaxed, they may end up saying things they would normally hold back or even behave in ways they would normally hide from the public. Therefore, when you observe people in an environment where they feel most relaxed, you might be able to see or hear their true thoughts and emotions.

- **How a person behaves when feeling stressed**

    This is another situation where you would see a person's true colors. When people are stressed out of their minds, they lose their ability to hide their true intentions or characteristics from others. During these peaks of heightened emotions, people may reveal dark and deep secrets. You might even be surprised to discover people who react positively to stressful situations, those who are able to persist despite the stress they feel.

- **How a person behaves when interacting with other people**

    Observe how people interact with others, as they may behave differently depending on the person they are interacting with. As you are analyzing others, you should observe their actions, behaviors, and the decisions they make throughout these interactions. You must learn how the person responds to people with varying educational backgrounds, cultures, social status, and more.

Also, observe how the person expresses themselves, behaves, and speaks to you. This shows you how they would interact with others too. For instance, if a person says a lot of negative things about other people who aren't present, they probably do the same when you're not around.

When you have observed a person in all of these scenarios, this will give you a clearer picture of who they really are. This is why analyzing others requires a lot of time, effort, reflection, and patience.

3. **Beliefs**

The beliefs of people also play a role in their actions, behaviors, and the decisions they make. These beliefs also determine what a person would be willing to do and what they will never agree to. One of the most significant aspects of people in terms of their beliefs is within the context of their religion. No matter what religion they have, they would be following a set of commandments, guidelines, rules or standards that they will abide by—because this is what's expected of them. Inevitably, when they end up breaking any of these rules, a person may suffer moral consequences or be faced with undesirable circumstances.

Because of the significance of religion, it would help you out a lot if you find out the religion of the person you are trying to analyze. After that, try to find out the person's level of conviction in terms of their religious beliefs. Having this information will help you come up with more accurate predictions of their thoughts, emotional patterns, and behaviors. Then you can use these predictions to influence them in the best way possible.

Significant as it is, religion is only one aspect of a person's beliefs. People may have other beliefs about work, love, life, play, self-expression, and more. All of these will help determine a person's actions, decision-making process, behaviors, and thoughts each and every day. As with any of the other building blocks of personality, the more thorough you are at gaining information about the beliefs of a person, the more you will be able to learn about their personalities and possible behaviors in the future.

4. **Goals and Objectives**

   Learning about the goals and objectives of a person would be like unlocking a vault that contains the things that motivate them and the things they consider as their priorities. While interacting with other people, try identifying these objectives while you search for common ground. This allows you to establish a deeper connection with the person which, in turn, allows you to get to know them better.

5. **Interests and Hobbies**

   These aspects of a person's life can help you learn more about their hierarchy of values. Upon learning the interests and hobbies of a person, you can effectively motivate or entice them. With this information, you can also come up with a plan that involves similar interests to make them more agreeable.

6. **Roles**

We all play certain roles throughout our life. These roles guide our behaviors, our thoughts, and how we live our lives in general. No matter what role a person plays, this comes with its own set of actions, emotions, decisions, beliefs, and a wide range of psychological characteristics. When a person is in the middle of playing a role, they would have their own behaviors compared to others who play different roles and have different responsibilities. Take these roles into consideration when analyzing others. Also, remember that the roles people play don't create them. These are another aspect of the entirety of the psychological makeup of a person. To analyze a person fully, you must be able to unlock all of these building blocks and more!

7. **Strengths and Weaknesses**

All people have two types of strengths and weaknesses—perceived ones and actual ones. Our perceived strengths and weaknesses are those that we recognized through our own perspectives. Of course, these are biased. The actual strengths and weaknesses are the ones we might not be aware of. In fact, those around us may be more aware of these than we are.

When you are interacting with others, you must learn how to differentiate a person's perceived and actual strengths and weaknesses. Learning how to make this distinction enables you to discover different characteristics of other people's personalities. You can determine the strengths and weaknesses of people through the things they say, their actions, gestures, and body language. For this, the key is to observe until you are able to identify these strengths and weaknesses. Then think about how you can use your new discovery to achieve your goals.

8. **Values**

   Just like a person's beliefs, learning the values of a person helps you unlock the actions, thoughts, emotions, and decision-making process of others so you can better predict how they may behave or think in the future. People have their own ranking system—an unconscious one—wherein they arrange the emotional experiences they have. The thing that people place on the very top rank is the one they value the most. This means that when they encounter an issue, they will most likely sacrifice the other things that are lower on their list for the sake of the thing they value the most. Knowing the values of a person will help you understand them more. Therefore, you should try to learn more about their hierarchy of values.

After you have learned all of these psychological building blocks of a person, you will have a better idea of who they are and what they stand for. Combine this information with everything else you have learned thus far and you are on your way to learning how to master the skill of analyzing others. But we're not done yet! There is still more to learn...

Analyzing Gestures and Body Language

The next thing to learn about is how to analyze the gestures and body language of other people. While the mind is more challenging because it is hidden, gestures and body language are more obvious because you can see them while you interact with others. Here are the things to observe:

Breathing Patterns

These breathing patterns refer to how deep a person breathes, the rhythm, and the rate of breathing. Observing all of these will provide you with insight into the hidden motives, behavior patterns, and thoughts of a person. For instance, if you are talking to someone who is taking short and quick breaths high in their chest, this may be an indication of anxiety and nervousness. Conversely, if the person you are talking to is taking slow and rhythmic breaths from their diaphragm, this may indicate that the person is carefree and relaxed. But if the deep breaths have a sporadic nature, this may indicate tension. Therefore, while you are analyzing others, take their breathing patterns into account.

Posture

A person's posture can provide you with a lot of clues about what is really in their mind. From how a person sits to how they walk, how they lean forward, and more—all of these things tell a story. Here are some examples of interpretations you could make based on a person's posture:

- When a person has poor posture, this may mean that they are harboring negative feelings or they don't have enough self-confidence.

- When you are talking to a person and they lean away from you, this may be because they are feeling stressed.
- When you are talking to a person and they lean back in a relaxed manner, this may indicate that they feel in-control or powerful.

Torso

When observing gestures and body language, observe the person's torso too. Generally, a person's attention goes toward the direction where their torso is pointing. This means that if a person's torso is faced toward you while talking, they are interested in what you have to say. Conversely, if a person's torso is pointed toward other directions, this indicates that they are disinterested in you and they might even want to end your interaction.

Eyes

We have already discussed how the eyes of a person can tell you a lot about them. Here are more things to look out for when you are observing this feature of a person:

- When a person sustains eye contact with you, this can indicate two things—that the person is lying or they are trying to dominate you.
- When a person uses "power gazing," they would only look at the point between your eyes—and this means that they are trying to avoid intimacy.
- When a person blinks quickly while talking to you, this may indicate that they are interested in you.
- When a person maintains eye contact for about 2 to 3 seconds then looks away, this indicates confidence. But if

the person is only able to sustain eye contact for a second (or less), this may indicate insecurity or evasion.
- When a person closes their eyes for some time, they may need time to think about what you have just said.

Ears

You might wonder why you would ever observe a person's ears while talking to them and how would this help you with your analysis. However, the most sophisticated readers believe that the ears can provide clues to a person's personality. Here are some things to look out for:

- A person with big ears may be spiritual and objective.
- A person with small ears may be determined and have excellent attention to detail.
- A person whose ears are high on their head may be a thinker and intellectual.
- A person whose ears stick out might be adventurous and always willing to try new things.

Smile

In particular, watch out for people who have fake smiles. There are several signs that may indicate that the smile of a person isn't authentic. For one, you may notice wrinkles around the eyes of a person when they smile genuinely, but not if the person's smile is fake. Here are some other things you can observe:

- People who smile authentically make use of more facial muscles than those who have fake smiles.
- Sometimes, fake smiles appear bigger as the person is trying to make this expression more obvious.

- Fake smiles actually look fake, especially when the person feels a lot of negativity towards you.

Hands

This part of the body can also provide you with important clues about the personality of a person or what a person is thinking. Here are some examples:

- When the person you're talking to is keeping their palms up, this may indicate that they are trying to "offer" you something, but it can also be an indication of submissiveness.
- When the person you're talking to is keeping their palms down, this may indicate that the person feels more powerful than you, but it may also indicate that something is being stopped or rejected.
- When the person you're talking to briefly touches your hand, this may indicate that they want to connect with you.
- When the person you're talking to tries hiding their hands, this may indicate that they are trying to hide other things from you.
- When the person you're talking to rubs their nose, this might indicate that they are lying to you.
- When the person you're talking to places their chin on their hand, this may indicate that they're trying to make a decision.
- When the person you're talking to scratches the back of their neck, this may indicate that their questions have not been answered yet.

Positive or negative body language

The body language of people can be categorized as positive or negative. By observing a person's body language, you can determine whether they feel positively or negatively towards you. Here are some examples of positive body language:

- When a person looks away from you in a shy way, this indicates positive emotions toward you.
- When a person doesn't cross their legs or arms while talking to you, this indicates positive feelings toward you.
- When a person leans toward you, this is also an indication of positive body language.

And here are some examples of negative body language:

- When a person points their feet toward the exit or away from you, this indicates that they have negative feelings toward you.
- When a person crosses their legs or arms, this may be an indication of wariness.
- When a person touches their eyes, nose or the back of their neck, this indicates that they have negative feelings toward you.
- When a person leans away from you or toward the side, this is also an indication of negative body language.

Movement Patterns

How people move their body can also help you determine what they're feeling and thinking. Observe the movement patterns of a person's body as they are communicating with or listening to you. Subtle as these signs are, these can provide you with important information about them, how they feel about you, and other non-verbal cues. We have already discussed different types of movements and what they may indicate. Now take all of these and try to see if a person has specific movement patterns while talking to you.

Overall Appearance

Finally, try to observe the overall appearance of a person. Are they dressed for success or are they wearing casual attire? Does the person's attire indicate power or a more laid-back, relaxed personality? Does it seem like the person takes pride in their appearance or not? All of these observations you make about the overall appearance of a person can say a lot about them.

Analyzing Words

The words people say and how they express these words can be powerful indicators you can use in your analysis. Don't just focus on the words themselves, but on the emotional content and meaning hidden behind those words. When it comes to analyzing words, here are some things to observe and keep in mind:

Voice tone and speed

When a person talks, the sounds they give off can reveal a lot about them. For voice tone and speed, here are some things you may discover about others:

- When you notice that a person's pitch suddenly changes, this might be an indication that they are lying.

- When people talk too much or too fast, this may be an indication of anxiety or insecurity.
- When people talk too slowly, this may be an indication that they lack spontaneity or that they are depressed.
- In particular, when men vary the tone of their voice while talking to a woman, this may indicate attraction.
- A tone that is repetitive may indicate insincerity.
- When a person sighs while talking, this may indicate frustration or sadness.

Emotional undertones of the person's words

The true motivations and intentions of people are normally hidden behind the words they say. With this fact in mind, pay close attention to the emotional undertones that lie behind the words used by other people. You can identify these undertones through a person's facial expressions, tone of voice, and body language as they communicate with you. Therefore, while talking to other people, make yourself aware of their whole person as this will give you a better picture of their psychological makeup. Only when you are able to see other people in their entirety will you be able to analyze them more effectively.

Choice of words

Of course, the words that people use in conversation will also provide you with clues about their behavior. For instance, if someone comes up to you to share news about you winning an award and they say it like, "Hey, you just won ANOTHER award," this statement would show that the person may have some level of insecurity or bitterness about the fact that they just shared with you. It shows the vulnerability of another person—and if you want to turn the situation around, you may want to thank the person and compliment them about something you know they are good at.

While considering the word choices of other people, try to observe if these words match their body language too. If you see any inconsistencies, there is a very high likelihood that they are not being entirely truthful with you. For most people, their choice of words reveals some parts of their personality such as:

- Their degrees and levels of exaggeration.
- Their personal biases regarding specific topics.
- Their hidden motives, agendas, and interests.
- Their ideas and opinions, both fictitious or factual.
- Their assumptions and misunderstandings.

When you can observe or catch the subtlest signs while talking to another person, this makes you more effective in terms of making adjustments to your strategies for conversing with them.

Length of sentences

On average, sentences contain between 10 to 15 words and this is called the "mean length of utterance." When a person uses sentences that are significantly shorter or longer, this may indicate that they are feeling stress. Also, some experts believe that when people deviate significantly from the mean length of utterance, this may be an indication that they are lying.

Words that may indicate that a person is lying

While it can be quite a challenge to tell for sure that a person is lying based on what they are saying, there are things you can observe to make a more accurate conclusion. For one, consider the comments a person makes along with the context of the situation.

While reading verbal cues isn't a foolproof way of identifying liars, here are some things that may indicate that a person isn't being completely truthful with you:

- When a person adds unnecessary qualifiers such as "to the best of my knowledge" or "from what I know," this may be an indication that they are lying.
- When a person answers your question by posing a question of their own, this may be an indication that they are trying to give themselves more time to come up with a story.
- When a person uses the present tense when referring to events that happened in the past, this may also be an indication that they are lying.
- When a person is lying, they might make use of words that soften the bad things or actions they are describing.
- When a person is lying, they may also avoid using the word "I" in order to take the focus away from themselves.

Silences

During conversations, the silences should not be ignored. In some cases, these silences reveal a lot of insights and information about a person. When you ask a question to a person, pay close attention to their answer along with anything they didn't mention or say, especially if you already have an idea of the answer to your question. While conversing, when a person pauses, pay close attention to their facial expressions and body language, too. This will give you insight into their emotional state and thinking patterns.

Pay Attention to Your Intuition

Beyond the words and actions of a person, you can still analyze other people through your intuition. Intuition refers to your "gut feeling," not to what your mind is saying. Your intuition is your way of tuning in to non-verbal information that you perceive through body knowings, images, ah-ha moments, and other abstract factors instead of the logical, concrete ones. In order to gain a complete understanding of other people, the important thing is to discover who the person really is, not just their outer persona. Your intuition allows you to see beyond what is in front of you in order to discover a much richer picture.

- **Be aware when you start feeling goosebumps**

    Goosebumps are considered "intuitive tingles" that convey the resonations we have with certain people. It's like these people have "struck a chord" with you and your intuition causes goosebumps to emerge. There are many instances where a person might cause you to feel goosebumps. When this happens, try to dig deeper in order to learn more about that person.

- **Pay attention and listen to your gut feelings**

    Whenever you have a gut feeling, listen to it. This is especially true when you meet people for the first time. These gut feelings are a visceral reaction you have that happens even before you can think about the situation and they help you feel whether you are at ease with the person or not. In other words, gut feelings are a primal response that occurs quickly. You can think of them as your very own truth meter to help you determine if you can trust a person or not.

- **Watch out for intuitive empathy**

    There are times when you may feel the emotions or physical symptoms of other people in your own body. This is a very intense type of empathy to watch out for. As you are trying to analyze others, notice whether you start feeling these symptoms or not. If you want to find out if what you're feeling is intuitive empathy, get feedback from them.

- **Pay attention when you experience flashes of insight**

    When you are conversing with others, you may also experience an "ah-ha!" moment that occurs in a flash. Be aware of these moments so you don't miss them. Again, when you are able to catch these flashes of insight, dig a little deeper so you can find out what caused them.

While you shouldn't just rely on first impressions, the fact is, these are usually pretty accurate. Since intuition plays an important role in your first impressions, you should pay attention to it. Accurate or not, the first impression you have about a person will have a huge impact on how you interact with them. If you want to change your impression about a person, you would have to consciously work hard to do it. Here are some pointers to keep in mind when it comes to your intuition and the first impressions you have about people:

- Try to watch out for "fake signals" people give for the purpose of manipulation. If you feel like there's something "off," don't trust the person just yet.
- If you notice that a person is doing behavioral or speech mimicry and you feel good when talking to this person, this may mean that you are emotionally in-sync
- Try to focus more on unconscious behaviors people make, those that they can't control easily but convey a very clear message.
- If you meet a person who you find attractive but your intuition is trying to tell you something else, listen carefully. This is because you might get distracted by your attraction to the other person and end up having an inaccurate first impression or analysis about them.
- Pay attention to the "visual identity claims" of others. These refer to the things a person displays to say something about how they want other people to perceive them. These identity claims are conscious statements people make about their values, goals, attitudes, and more. Since people consciously choose them, interpreting these can give you a pretty accurate analysis of who the person is and what they are all about.
- If you meet a person and your intuition says that they are confident, conscientious, religious or extroverted, chances are, you're right!
- If you find someone to be really funny, this may indicate that they are smart as well. This is especially true if the person is witty and they appeal to your inner humorous side.
- If you think that a person is honest and warm, try to pay attention to how much they use the word "I." Those who use this word often are more honest and warm while those

who don't use it as much tend to be more confident in themselves.
- The most important thing to pay attention to when it comes to your intuition or gut feelings is when you are feeling threatened or unsafe. If you are alone with a person and you have these feelings, find a way to get yourself out of the situation in a calm and subtle way.

When it comes to using intuition and gut feelings for your analysis, the bottom line is very simple... pay attention!

Chapter 8: Things to Avoid while Analyzing Other People

When it comes to analyzing other people, there are certain things you must avoid in order to improve the accuracy of your analysis. Of course, your main goal here is to come up with an accurate picture of a person based on what you have observed and your interpretations based on all of the tips we have discussed in the past chapters. But analyzing others isn't a perfect process. In fact, as you practice analyzing, you might discover new tips and tricks that you find very effective. You might also discover that some of the tips we have gone through here don't work as well as you would have hoped. Mastering this skill takes a lot of practice, experimentation, and learning. You also need a lot of time and patience to become as good as the experts. With that being said, here are some of the mistakes to avoid while analyzing other people.

Over-Analyzing

A lot of people tend to overanalyze situations—more than they will admit to themselves and to others. Although this may be helpful in some situations, it won't improve the skill you are trying to learn. The main reason for this is that overanalyzing might cause your mind to race or wander, thus moving you away from your goals. If you over-analyze each person you meet, you might end up feeling overwhelmed with all of the information running through your mind. This will cause you to lose focus, miss important details, and forget everything you have learned about non-verbal and subtle cues.

But how do you know that you are already overanalyzing?

One main sign that you are overanalyzing situations and people is that you can't seem to turn off your brain no matter how exhausted you feel. Even if you don't really aim to analyze a person, your mind immediately picks up things, explores them, and dissects all of the details. Even if your goal is to rest or focus on other tasks, you end up looking at everyone around you while trying to analyze who they are. When you try to distract your mind or bring back your focus to the task at hand, this requires tremendous effort.

Yes, you need to practice this skill—but this doesn't mean that it should overtake your entire life. Unless your job requires you to analyze people all day and come up with comprehensive reports about them, you need to consciously pull yourself back to more important matters. Although this isn't as easy as it may seem, allowing yourself to overanalyze everyone around you might end up making you mad! So take a break from it and only "turn it on" as needed. In fact, teaching yourself to become more aware will help hone the skill you are aiming to acquire.

Analysis Paralysis

By definition, analysis paralysis is a kind of anti-pattern or a state wherein a person over-analyzes a situation so much that they end up not taking any action; it is like they are paralyzed. When you experience analysis paralysis, you end up getting so lost in the process that you can't even make a decision. To help you better understand this state, let's first examine the normal process of how people make decisions. According to experts, this process can happen in two ways:

- Some people **maximize** wherein they don't like settling with available or obvious solutions. Instead, they keep searching for other alternatives that they think are better.
- Other **satisfice** wherein they choose the very first option that comes their way as long as it meets their requirements or needs. They don't bother with other alternatives as they feel satisfied with that first option.

Of course, when it comes to having an inability to make decisions, the first group is guilty of this—and they are usually the ones who end up suffering from analysis paralysis. Apart from maximizing, other reasons that may cause people to suffer from this state of paralysis are:

- Over-analyzing because you are faced with too many choices and you cannot process everything all at once.
- Over-analyzing in order to avoid making the wrong choice which, in turn, might end up in failure.

The good news is, you can work to overcome or prevent analysis paralysis. Now that you know that this state exists, you can become more aware of it. Then, you can take these steps:

- **Determine the goals you have for the decision you need to make**

  With a clear goal in mind, you will be able to better determine what decision or option to choose. In terms of analyzing other people, think about what you want to get out of your interactions. If you need to influence their decision in your favor, use your analysis to determine the ones who are most likely to side with you. With your goals in mind along with the analysis tips you have already learned, you can look out for specific behaviors or gestures to help you determine who to work on more closely. This will help increase your success in influencing others.

- **Breakdown the decisions you need to make into smaller parts**

  After identifying your goals, it's time to analyze them. Going back to the same situation in the previous point, your goal is to influence a lot of people to side with you (no matter what decision you need to make). For this situation, how do you break the steps down? Well, you can first make a list of the people whom you think are already most inclined to side with you. Talk to these people first. Once you have their votes, you can start talking to the other people in your workplace. To help you determine who may or may not side with you, observe the people in the office (this time with a specific purpose in mind) and analyze their behaviors. The more you can break down the decisions you need to make, the easier you will be able to make a choice.

- **Don't expect perfection from yourself and from other people**

    If you end up making the wrong decision—like if you started by trying to convince an entire group of people who ended up deciding against your favor—brush it off and learn from your mistake. Don't expect yourself to come up with an accurate analysis of everyone around you each time, especially at the beginning. Forgive yourself when you make mistakes and this will help ease your tendency to overanalyze then end up with analysis paralysis.

For this particular issue, the bottom line is to become more aware of how your mind works, how you analyze, and how you can use this skill to help you make a decision instead of hindering you from it. If you want to avoid analysis paralysis, don't allow yourself to get overwhelmed. If you feel like you are starting to get overwhelmed, take a step back, sort out your thoughts, and bring your focus back to your main goal.

Things to be Careful of When Analyzing Other People

How wonderful would it be if you could analyze other people as easily as Sherlock Holmes solved mysteries? While you still have a long journey ahead of you, with the right knowledge and enough practice, who's to say that this isn't possible?

After learning about the two main mistakes of analyzing others (over-analyzing and analysis paralysis), the next mistakes for you to avoid have something to do with body language. These are:

- **You're not taking your biases into consideration**

    There are some cases when you meet a person and, for some reason, you just dislike them immediately. Unfortunately, with your biases affecting your first impression of a person, you should know that this will also have an effect on how you analyze them. The same case happens when you have already gotten to know a person and you don't like them. This dislike or negativity will unconsciously sway your analysis and the results you come up with. When it comes to analyzing other people, try to eliminate your biases in order to come up with a more objective analysis and a more accurate result.

- **You aren't trying to observe clusters**

    This is one of the biggest mistakes you can make when analyzing others—trying to look for just one behavior or "tell." While this might work in movies, when it comes to real life, it's more effective to observe clusters of behaviors. Taking these together would be a more accurate predictor of what a person is really thinking or feeling.

- **You're not considering the context or situation**

    While all of the gestures we had already discussed can have several interpretations, you must also consider the context in which your interactions have happened. For instance, if you're talking in a very cold room and the person you are talking to crossed their arms, this might just mean that they are feeling cold. In order to avoid this mistake, the best thing you can do is use your common sense. As you are observing the other person, try to be aware of your situation, environment, and context as well.

- **You haven't created a baseline**

    Remember the baseline that was introduced in Chapter 5? Well, one of the biggest mistakes you can make while observing other people and analyzing their actions, words or behaviors is not coming up with a baseline. Without it, how will you know if the person displays any deviations? After meeting a new person for the first time, you should start working on creating their baseline to serve as your guide for future observations and analyses.

Apart from body language, observing the behaviors of other people can help you analyze them more effectively. In this aspect, there are also some common mistakes people make that make them inefficient at analyzing others. As you analyze the people you interact with, avoid these mistakes:

- **You interpret their behavior through your personal perspectives**

    Keep in mind that we all have our own reasons for behaving the way we do. But when one person behaves the same way as you, that doesn't mean that they have the same reason for it. When a person shows the same behaviors as you, don't get too excited. Try to dig deeper so you can determine the reasons why a person is behaving just like you.

    Never interpret behaviors through your own personal perspectives, as you won't end up with an accurate analysis. Instead, learn more about the person you are talking to and try to see if these behaviors are common to them. They might just be mirroring you or the behaviors you have observed are deviations from how they really are or what they really do.

- **You don't understand that the motives behind behaviors aren't always clear**

When it comes to interpreting motives, you should understand that distortions in motives can happen for a number of reasons. Behaviors themselves are easy to observe, but not the psychological markers driving those behaviors. Analyzing other people is a complicated process. Sometimes, the behaviors people manifest are those which they want other people to see to make them look better than who or what they really are.

If you truly want to interpret behaviors, you should also try to discover and analyze the motives that drive these behaviors. Don't expect things to be easy and clear all the time. The more you are able to dig deeper and discover what's behind these behaviors, the more you will learn about the people you are trying to analyze.

- **You don't think a person's personality and character will affect their motives**

Often, a person's character and personality are far more enduring than their motives. But this doesn't mean that you can use a person's character and personality to accurately determine the motives behind a person's behaviors. Although you can use the personality of a person as your basis to predict what they will do in specific situations, motives have an integrative nature that may disrupt the predictive aspect of personality.

There are other factors that may override the normal behavior patterns of people. For instance, when an introvert meets someone at a party who shares the same interests then suddenly comes alive. The point here is that you should try to avoid labeling people according to their "motivational type." Unlike personalities, motives are more variable and malleable. They tend to fluctuate based on environmental and social factors apart from a person's dominant characteristics or personality.

- **You don't take a person's emotions into account**

Emotions play a huge role in how people behave. Without taking a person's emotions into account, you might end up making false interpretations of their motives. Keep in mind that people who are feeling emotional strain may experience changes in their response patterns. When a person's mind gives in to the perception of strong emotions, this causes normative psychological and physiological patterns to change based on the most prevalent emotions.

When meeting or interacting with others, try to ask about what they are feeling and include this in your analysis. You can also try to observe how the other person is feeling if you don't want to ask about this directly. The important thing is to discover a person's emotions as this will help you learn more about them.

- **You think certain behaviors always represent the same motives**

  Finally, don't think that certain behaviors always mean the same thing. As previously mentioned, a person might have different reasons for their behaviors. Even if two different people display the same behaviors or actions, don't think they mean the same thing. Again, it's better for you to dig deeper and try to learn more so you can come up with a more accurate conclusion.

Chapter 9:
Learning How to Analyze Yourself

As part of your journey of learning how to analyze people, you must also learn how to analyze yourself. By definition, self-analysis is making yourself consciously aware of yourself. It means that you make yourself aware of your own strengths, weaknesses, capabilities, and surroundings. It means making yourself aware of who you are in your entirety. In order to analyze yourself successfully, you must make a conscious effort to do so.

Self-analysis is one of the first steps you must take toward enlightenment. Learning more about yourself through analysis allows you to have a clearer mind when it's time to start analyzing others. Each day, we act in unconscious ways as we live our lives that we don't even know that we are doing it. We simply respond to what happens around us. Unfortunately, when you act this way, this means that you aren't a conscious person. But when you analyze yourself consciously, you will gain a more profound understanding of yourself, how you behave, why you are the way you are, and what truly matters to you. Self-analysis is an important part of the process which is why you should also learn how to do this correctly.

Understanding Yourself First

Analyzing others is a skill that can help improve your life in so many ways. Self-analysis is another important skill that allows you to get to know yourself better while making yourself aware of your own thoughts, feelings, behaviors, and personality. When you know yourself better, you don't have to be caught off-guard when someone else is trying to analyze you. Here are the most important benefits you can get from self-analysis:

- The more you understand who you are, the more you will be able to understand other people while you are analyzing them. For instance, if you are a confident person, you would know where your confidence in yourself originates. You would also understand how it feels to lack confidence as you would have already felt this in the past. This knowledge can help you deal with a person whom you have observed lacks this trait. In other words, having a good understanding of your own traits allows you to connect with other people more.
- Self-analysis helps you find yourself which, in turn, won't make you feel "lost" in life. Since you know who you are and what you are all about, you would also know where you belong. In terms of relationships, career, and other aspects, you will have a clearer idea of where you should be and work toward that.
- When you know yourself, you will be able to know the exact reasons behind what you are feeling. You won't have to feel bothered without really knowing why. In turn, this helps you determine the steps to take in order to improve your feelings and find happiness.

- Self-analysis can also help improve your moods. While this won't solve all of your problems, learning how to improve your mood will help you adopt a more positive attitude. With this positive attitude, you can increase your productivity, face problems head-on, and make your life better in different ways.

Self-analysis is truly beneficial. If you have been wanting to improve your life through analysis, starting with yourself may just be the key to unlocking this particular challenge you are facing.

The Importance of Analyzing Yourself

Apart from helping you become more effective at analyzing other people, self-analysis enables you to assess and understand your passions, interests, strengths, weaknesses, priorities, values, and skills. Analyzing yourself helps you explore your past, determine where you are now, and create your path to the future you want for yourself. This process is truly important and in order to do this, here are some things for you to consider:

- **Consider taking psychometric tests**

    There are so many psychometric tests that you can take online. These can provide you with some valuable insight into the different aspects of your personality. These tests are objective and if you will apply for a job, you may have to take them as well. However, when it comes to such tests, don't believe everything you read. While there are legit tests available out there, a lot of the online tests are only meant for amusement. Still, you can use the results from these tests to discover more about yourself and see if those results match the analysis you have already made about yourself.

- **Your self-analysis may help you if you're planning to make a change in your life**

   Analyzing yourself is particularly significant when you want to make a huge change in your life such as a change in your career. There must be a reason why you want to make a change, right? You can discover that reason through self-analysis. Before taking any steps toward making a change, analyze yourself. Understand your reason behind the change and use what you have discovered about yourself to come up with a plan for implementing that change.

- **You can also use your analysis to evaluate your transferable skills**

   As you analyze yourself, you will also be able to understand your skills more. In doing this, you can determine what you can do, what you want to do, and if your skills will allow you to do what you want to do. The more you learn about yourself and your skills, the more you can use this knowledge to move forward with all the plans you have made for yourself.

How to Analyze Yourself

As you can see, analyzing yourself is of the utmost importance. Although you cannot truly know yourself (specifically the deepest, subconscious aspects of your personality), learning as much as you can through analysis can benefit your life in so many ways. If you're wondering how you can analyze yourself, here are some tips to help you out:

1. **Give meditation a try**

    By definition, meditation refers to a wide range of practices and techniques that are meant to build your internal energy, promote relaxation, and develop positive characteristics. Simple as this practice may seem, if you make it a regular part of your life, it will help you learn more about yourself. The great thing about meditation is that it doesn't require a lot of time, it's easy to learn, and there are so many resources online to help you out. Making meditation part of your self-analysis will help transform you into a person with endless possibilities.

2. **Try the SWOT Analysis**

    SWOT stands for Strength, Weakness, Opportunity, Threats. This method of analysis is a basic tool that businesses use—and you can also use it to learn more about yourself. Through SWOT Analysis, you can determine your strengths (the things you excel at) and your weaknesses (the things you find challenging to do). Knowing these can help you use your strengths more effectively and work on your weaknesses to help improve them. Then you can start searching for opportunities where you can use your strengths while trying to remove the threats that come with your weaknesses. While performing this analysis, you must maintain an open mind. There is no point in doing the SWOT analysis when you can't accept your weaknesses. Remember, your goal here is to learn as much as you can about yourself in order to improve your life!

3. Evaluate your level of self-esteem

Self-esteem is an important part of our life. Without it, you might end up getting paralyzed with fear whenever you are faced with difficult situations. Think about your level of self-esteem now—is it enough to enable you to interact with others and analyze them accurately? If you lack self-esteem, you might doubt yourself at every turn. Of course, this isn't helpful. Try to work on building your self-esteem. Surround yourself with positive people, do things that make you happy, and focus on the things you are good at. Over time, you may notice your self-esteem improving and when this happens, you can start learning more about those around you

4. Assess your patterns of thinking

A huge part of analyzing others is thinking about what you have observed and coming up with conclusions. If you want to be effective at analyzing others, you should learn more about your own patterns of thinking. If needed, you can try maintaining a journal where you write down your thoughts throughout the day. After some time, you can examine what you have written down and try to notice any patterns in your thinking. Determine the underlying theme of your thoughts—are they positive, liberating, and healthy or are your thoughts mostly self-defeating and pessimistic? Of course, if it's the latter, it's time for you to start changing your thought patterns.

5. Determine your personality type

Most people fall within 5 major personality types. One aspect of self-analysis is to determine which of these personality types you belong to. For this, you need to do a lot of reflection and interpretation. The major personality types are:

- **Agreeableness**

    These people are caring, empathic, and are able to understand how other people feel easily. They are tender-hearted, nice, and can sometimes be driven by their emotions.

- **Conscientiousness**

    These people always consider the feelings of others before they make a decision. They have a high level of self-control, they are well-organized, disciplined, and do well with autonomy.

- **Extroversion**

    These people have a keen interest in external events and the people around them. They are confident and highly adventurous. By contrast, introversion is when a person prefers to be alone and thrive in quiet environments.

- **Neuroticism**

    These people always have some level of anxiety. They have a tendency to possess negative emotions. They worry excessively and tend to freak out when they feel like the situation is going beyond their control.

○ **Openness**

These people are always willing to change their thoughts and opinions when presented with new information. They are free-spirited, unconventional, and accept others for who they are.

While you may not fall into just one of these main personality traits, think about the one you relate to the most. When you know which group you belong to, you can consider these as your strengths. Then think about which personality traits you may lack (the positive ones at least) and you can start working on improving them.

6. Ask for help from others

Finally, you can improve your self-analysis by asking for help from others. You may learn a lot about yourself, but asking other people to describe yourself for you will give you more insight into who you really are. Talk to your family members, friends, and even your acquaintances. Tell them that you are in the process of analyzing yourself and encourage them to be as honest as possible with you (it would help to reassure them that you won't hold anything against them). Make a note of what people say about you, then compare this with the information you have gathered about yourself. Combining all of this information will give you a pretty accurate analysis of who you are as a person!

Chapter 10:
Becoming a Master at Analyzing People

Learning how to analyze people doesn't happen overnight. It may take a long time for you to become a true master of this skill. But one thing's for sure, gaining proficiency in this skill isn't an impossible task. By now, you have already learned everything you need to start becoming more aware, observant, and reflective. Upon meeting someone new or even when you are trying to come up with an analysis of someone you have already known for a while now, applying everything you have learned in this book will help you out immensely.

In order to become better at analyzing people, you should remember what you have learned here, observe people carefully, and try to come up with conclusions, interpretations, and analyses based on your observations and interactions with others. In this final chapter, we will have a recap of everything you have learned from the beginning in order to help with your understanding of the process of how to analyze other people.

Basic Steps to Help You Out

One huge part of analyzing others is learning how to be perceptive about thoughts and feelings. This is an essential skill you must develop in order to communicate better and navigate your interpersonal relationships more effectively. One person may vary greatly from another but at the very core, we are all wired in a similar way. We have discussed so many things to help you analyze others better but at the beginning, you can follow a simple process with basic steps to make it easier for you. Over time, as you learn how to be more observant, more aware, and as you learn how to interpret and analyze while observing, then you can start refining your process of analysis to make it more efficient. As you begin, here are some basic steps for you to follow:

1. **Get to know the person**

    One of the most important steps for analyzing others is to come up with a baseline for each person. To do this, you must get to know the person better. While you can analyze others even if you don't know them well, your analysis of the person might be fairly shallow as well. But the more you get to know someone, the more you will be able to build a strong baseline which, in turn, helps with your analysis.

    Observe how a person interacts with you and with others around them. Pay attention to their habits as well. While talking to others, ask them a lot of open-ended questions. The answers to these questions will provide you with more insight as to who a person is and what a person is all about. After establishing a baseline, try to determine if you observe any inconsistencies. In such a case, you may try to find out why these consistencies have happened to give you a better understanding of how they have affected the person.

2. **Listen to what the person has to say**

   Always go beyond what a person is saying when you are trying to analyze them. Listen to their tone, volume, the words they use, and the emotions behind their message. All of these will help you learn more about the true thoughts and feelings of a person. Also, take note of how long the person's responses are. These will tell you whether a person is enjoying your interaction or not. Basically, when it comes to what a person has to say, you must start with what you hear and go beyond this to get the entire message the other person is trying to convey.

3. **Carefully observe a person's body language**

   Take a look at how a person holds themselves. A person's body language will provide you with a wealth of information to use in your analysis. This may be a reflection of an interpersonal issue the person is experiencing or a reaction to the topic of your conversation. There are comfortable and positive cues for body language including relaxed limbs, leaning forward, eye contact, a genuine smile, and more. There are also uncomfortable and negative cues for body language including crossed arms, looking away while talking to you, leaning away from you, stiff limbs, and more. Try to observe these cues to give you a better idea of how they feel about your interaction.

   While talking to someone or while observing them when they are interacting with others, observe the person's face carefully. See their expressions, the movements of the parts of their face, and even facial expressions that come and go in a matter of seconds. The things that go on in a person's face will also tell you a lot about what they really mean or what they really want to say. From their eyes, mouth, eyebrows, and all the other parts of their face, all of these things say a lot.

As part of their body language, try to observe how close or far a person stands from you or from other people. This will also help indicate how comfortable or uncomfortable the person is feeling. Also, try to observe whether the person touches you in some way throughout the conversation. When it comes to body language, observing in clusters is especially important.

4. **Observe and analyze a person in different situations and contexts**

Finally, don't just base your analysis on a single encounter. Just as you would observe how a person interacts with others, you should also observe a person while in different situations, environments, and contexts. People often act differently when faced with different situations. For instance, when a person meets someone they are attracted to, they may exhibit different behaviors toward that person compared to a person they don't find attractive or interesting.

As you observe a person in different contexts and environments, take note of the behaviors, gestures, and body language you see. Then try to compare all of these with the baseline you have created for the person. Through this comparison, you can come up with an interpretation of who the person is along with all of their different aspects.

This step can also help you determine if a person is lying or not. For instance, while talking to a person, you may observe that they are comfortable with you, they smile a lot, and they share a lot of information with you. But if they are faced with a person whom you know they are trying to hide something from, you will definitely notice deviations in their normal behavior. Now take this concept and apply it to when a person is acting nervous or fidgety around you. The more you observe people in different situations, the more you learn about them and the more you can predict their actions, thoughts, and feelings both at present and in the future.

How Do You Know That You're Good at Analyzing People?

After some time, you can check your own progress to find out if you are improving or not. When you discover that you are getting better at analyzing people, you will feel more motivated to keep going, keep learning, and keep practicing. If you think that you haven't made progress (which is highly unlikely), then you can review this book and try to see where you might have gone wrong, what you might have missed, or what you can do to improve yourself and start to get the ball rolling. If you want to know if you are already good at this skill, here are some indications:

- The first time you meet a person, you would have a very strong intuition about them and you can't explain this feeling logically. Through this first meeting, you can already tell whether the person is worth getting to know better or not.

- When a person is upset, you can tell right away even if they keep telling everyone that they are fine. Despite their reassurances, you can tell that there is something bothering them.
- Your intuition goes beyond people. You have enhanced it so much that you can start using your intuition to get out of harmful or dangerous situations.
- Whenever you enter a relationship with someone, you can tell whether it will only last for a short time or it will last long. This is because you have analyzed your partner while getting to know them better.
- While reading books or watching movies, you are able to predict how the story will go or if there will be any twists to the story's plot.
- You can accurately guess the true feelings and thoughts of a person even though they are trying to hide these.
- While chatting or sending text messages with other people, you can somehow tell what tone the other person is using.
- You are very good at detecting liars. You can always tell if someone is lying or being truthful.
- At some point, all people start becoming predictable to you. Even before they tell you something or share something with you, you would already have an idea about what it is.
- You are very effective at communicating and interacting with other people from all walks of life. You are able to determine what makes them tick, thus, you already know what they are thinking and feeling.

What Can You Expect After You Master This Skill?

After mastering this skill of analyzing other people, you can start applying it to all aspects of your life. You can use the skill in your home life, at work, with your friends, and so on. For instance, if you're looking for a nanny or babysitter to watch over your children at home, you can use this skill to analyze each and every person you are interviewing. This is essential, as you will be placing the safety and well-being of your children in the hands of this person. Therefore, when you interview different candidates, use your skill of analyzing others to make sure that you choose the best person for the job.

In your professional life, you can use this skill to better communicate and interact with your colleagues, superiors, and even your bosses. If you need to influence them, analyzing them first will help you come up with a better way of doing this to ensure that you achieve the results you are aiming for. Basically, applying this skill actively in the different aspects of your life will help you out in so many ways! After all, this is the main reason why you wanted to learn the skill in the first place, right?

Conclusion:
It's Time to Start Learning More About the People Around You

There you have it! Everything you need to know about analyzing the people around you. From start to finish, you have just learned all the fundamental information to help you ask the right questions, make the right observations, and come up with the right interpretations to help you learn everything you can about a person. As previously mentioned, this skill is not an easy one to learn. It does take a lot of time, conscious effort, practice, and patience to master.

Of course, there's no time to start like the present! Now that you are armed with all of this new, enriching information, you can start applying the knowledge you have gained to your life. With each person you meet and encounter every day of your life, you can practice this skill. Then when the time comes where you need to seriously analyze someone for a specific purpose, then you can use this skill again to help you out. As with any other skill, analyzing others requires a lot of practice. The more you do it, the more it becomes automatic for you. While all of this information may seem overwhelming and confusing right now, as long as you use it over and over again, it will become a part of your normal thinking.

Soon, you will realize that you have become better at analyzing others. You are more aware of your surroundings, you are more observant while interacting with others, and you are already able to interpret the things you are observing as you observe them. Make it your goal to practice and improve yourself. Only then will you be able to reap the fruits of your labor. Good luck!

References

6 Signs You Over Analyze Everything. (2016). Retrieved from https://www.higherperspectives.com/over-analyze-1769157720.html

20+ Psychological Tricks That Can Help You Read People Like Open Books. (2019). Retrieved from https://brightside.me/inspiration-tips-and-tricks/20-psychological-tricks-that-will-help-you-read-people-like-open-books-416260/

Alessandra, T. How to Read the 4 Most Common Personality Types. (2017). Retrieved from https://www.success.com/the-skill-youve-always-wanted-how-to-instantly-read-people/

Bariso, J. An FBI Agent Shares 9 Secrets to Reading People. (2018). Retrieved from https://www.inc.com/justin-bariso/an-fbi-agents-9-ways-to-read-people.html

Barker, E. How to become an expert in reading other people. (2016). Retrieved from https://theweek.com/articles/634045/how-become-expert-reading-other-people

Bhasin, K. 18 Tips And Tricks About Reading People. (2011). Retrieved from https://www.businessinsider.com/tips-on-how-to-read-people-2011-6#learning-how-to-read-people-must-occur-over-time-a-weeklong-crash-course-wont-cut-it-17

Campbell, S. Understanding the Other Person's Perspective Will Radically Increase Your Success. (2016). Retrieved from https://www.entrepreneur.com/article/275543

Cooper, O. Relationships: Do Some People Analyse Others In Order To Avoid Themselves?. (2019). Retrieved from https://www.selfgrowth.com/articles/relationships-do-some-people-analyse-others-in-order-to-avoid-themselves

Demographic Factors to Consider | Boundless Communications. (2019). Retrieved from https://courses.lumenlearning.com/boundless-communications/chapter/demographic-factors-to-consider/

Grabowski, P. Analysis Paralysis: What It Is and How to Avoid It | UserVoice Blog. (2019). Retrieved from http://community.uservoice.com/blog/analysis-paralysis-what-it-is-and-how-to-avoid-it/

Herman, L. Are You Really as Good at Reading People as You Think?. (2019). Retrieved from https://www.themuse.com/advice/are-you-really-as-good-at-reading-people-as-you-think

Hoffman, B. 5 pitfalls to understanding people's motives. (2015). Retrieved from https://www.elsevier.com/connect/5-pitfalls-to-understanding-peoples-motives

How to analyze people. (2011). Retrieved from https://hubpages.com/education/How-to-analyze-people

How to Conduct a Self Analysis. (2019). Retrieved from https://www.wikihow.com/Conduct-a-Self-Analysis

How to Profile People. (2019). Retrieved from https://www.wikihow.com/Profile-People

How to Read a Person. (2019). Retrieved from https://www.wikihow.com/Read-a-Person

How to Read People. (2019). Retrieved from https://www.wikihow.com/Read-People

How To Read People: 5 Secrets Backed By Research - Barking Up The Wrong Tree. (2019). Retrieved from https://www.bakadesuyo.com/2016/06/how-to-read-people-2/

How Self-Analysis is Important for Success and How to do it. (2019). Retrieved from http://leadtogrow.blogspot.com/2015/11/how-self-analysis-is-important.html

Hurst, K. How To Stop Overanalyzing Everything And Overcome Worrying. (2019). Retrieved from http://www.thelawofattraction.com/stop-analyzing-everything/

Iskarius, J. How To Analyze People On Sight. (2018). Retrieved from https://iskarius.com/2018/08/29/how-to-analyze-people-on-sight/

Jeary, T. This Is How You Can Get Better at Reading People. (2018). Retrieved from https://www.success.com/this-is-how-you-can-get-better-at-reading-people/

McAneny, B. Why is it important to understand personality?. (2014). Retrieved from https://preludecharacteranalysis.com/blog/why-is-it-important-to-understand-personality

Orloff, J. Three Techniques to Read People. (2014). Retrieved from https://www.psychologytoday.com/us/blog/emotional-freedom/201402/three-techniques-read-people

Ostdick, J. How to Understand People's Personality Types. (2015). Retrieved from https://www.success.com/how-to-understand-peoples-personality-types/

Perrine, J. The Benefits of Understanding Personality Types in the Workplace | All Things Admin. (2019). Retrieved from https://www.allthingsadmin.com/benefits-understanding-personality-types-workplace/

Radwan, F. How to analyze someone's personality | 2KnowMySelf. (2019). Retrieved from https://www.2knowmyself.com/how_to_analyze_someone_personality

Radwan, M. How to understand someone's mind | 2KnowMySelf. (2019). Retrieved from https://www.2knowmyself.com/How_to_understand_someone_mind

Radwan, M. How to Understand Yourself And Others | 2KnowMySelf. (2019). Retrieved from https://www.2knowmyself.com/Self_understanding/know_yourself/How_to_understand_yourself_and_others

Reidbord, S. Do You Analyze Everyone You Meet?. (2011). Retrieved from https://www.psychologytoday.com/us/blog/sacramento-street-psychiatry/201109/do-you-analyze-everyone-you-meet

Riordan, H. 10 Signs You Are Exceptionally Good At Reading People. (2018). Retrieved from https://thoughtcatalog.com/holly-riordan/2018/03/10-signs-you-are-exceptionally-good-at-reading-people/

Sicinski, A. Unlocking Personality: Learn How to Read People Like an FBI Profiler. (2019). Retrieved from https://blog.iqmatrix.com/unlock-personality

The Critical 7 Rules To Understand People | Scott H Young. (2007). Retrieved from https://www.scotthyoung.com/blog/2007/08/28/the-critical-7-rules-to-understand-people/

The Importance Of Conducting A Self Analysis | Renovo UK. (2019). Retrieved from https://renovo.uk.com/importance-conducting-self-analysis/

Three Types of Audience Analysis. (2019). Retrieved from https://saylordotorg.github.io/text_stand-up-speak-out-the-practice-and-ethics-of-public-speaking/s08-02-three-types-of-audience-analys.html

What Our Faces Reveal About Our Personality | Science of People. (2019). Retrieved from https://www.scienceofpeople.com/face-personality/

www.ingramcontent.com/pod-product-compliance
Lightning Source LLC
Chambersburg PA
CBHW031157020426
42333CB00013B/712